Longaberger®
FRESH FROM THE PANTRY
RECIPES *for* EVERY DAY

This cookbook is a collection of favorite recipes,
which are not necessarily original recipes.
Published by The Longaberger® Company.

FRESH FROM THE PANTRY
RECIPES FOR EVERY DAY

Copyright© 2001 by
The Longaberger® Company
1500 East Main Street
Newark, Ohio 43055-8847

Food Photographer: Paul Poplis
Cover and Location Photographs: Colin McGuire
Food Stylists: Sharon Reiss, Julie Garber and Mary Leber

Food Consultant and Stylist: Sharon Reiss
Creative Consultant: Keith Keegan
Illustrations: Nora Corbett
Writer: Mary Douglas

Library of Congress Catalog Number: 2001126205
ISBN: 0-9701813-2-9

Edited, Designed, and Manufactured by
Favorite Recipes® Press
an imprint of

FRP

P.O. Box 305142
Nashville, Tennessee 37230
800-358-0560

Managing Editor: Mary Cummings
Art Director: Steve Newman
Book Project Manager: Linda A. Jones

Manufactured in the United States of America
First Printing: 2001

Longaberger®
FRESH FROM THE PANTRY
RECIPES *for* EVERY DAY

WELCOME TO THE LONGABERGER® PANTRY

A tiny house in Dresden, Ohio, was home to our founder, Dave Longaberger, and his eleven brothers and sisters. Dave's mom, our "Grandma Bonnie," and his dad, J.W. Longaberger, surely had their hands full in what was no doubt a very noisy house. Yet crowded as it was, we know theirs was also a home where love lived, and where true sit-down, home-cooked meals brought the whole family together each day.

If your family is like the Longaberger's, you too know the value of sitting down together to share great food, news of the day, school gossip, silly jokes, and carefree laughter. You also know that here is the place to share dreams—one of Dave's passions in life—because shared dreams are one of the surest ways to stay close as the years roll on.

In this spirit of family togetherness, Longaberger brings you *Fresh from the Pantry, Recipes for Every Day.* Within its 192 pages you'll find a collection of classic American recipes that are simple to make and easy to love. All of the ingredients can be found year-round at the grocery store. And to borrow from one of Dave's favorite lines, just about all of these recipes come to you "subject to change." In other words, try the main recipe or vary it, according to any of the effortless yet exciting variations listed alongside it. Have fun reinventing new recipes each time you revisit the book!

Our "What's in Your Pantry?" section is filled with common sense advice on stocking your larder. Put into practice, you'll find it much easier to whip up last-minute meals, kid-friendly snacks, and memorable feasts for impromptu guests. You'll also find all kinds of indispensable tips and innovative ideas to make your job as family chef ever more efficient and enjoyable.

And of course, we wouldn't be Longaberger if we didn't also suggest a few ways to maximize the use of our heirloom-quality baskets, pottery, wrought iron pieces, and kitchen linens. You'll find them a big help keeping your pantry and kitchen organized, and a joy to use in preparing and presenting the mouth-watering favorites found in the pages ahead.

All of us in the Longaberger family (and there are now thousands of us!) dedicate this book to your family in the hope that these recipes will be warmly welcomed at your table, adding to lively conversations, the sharing of love, and the building of many dreams.

Our goal? "To stimulate a better quality of life." It's really as simple as that.

CONTENTS

WHAT'S IN YOUR PANTRY? 8

SHALL WE START? 26

WHAT'S FOR DINNER? 62

What's in Your Pantry?

Until the first part of the 20th century, most American homes had a small room adjacent to the kitchen known as the "larder" or "pantry." It was generally used to house whatever was needed in the kitchen, be it food, cooking implements, or serving pieces. Later in the century, kitchens were fitted with built-in cupboards, shelves, drawers, refrigerators, and freezers. The result is that, in today's homes, the entire kitchen is the pantry! Everyone's kitchen is arranged differently, of course, but one thing is certain: A well-stocked and organized "pantry" makes for much more efficient meal planning, streamlined grocery shopping, and healthier, more interesting meals. If you've ever found yourself panicked about a last-minute meal, you'll understand the value of a pantry that provides you with plenty of tempting choices on short notice. America's supermarkets are filled with an amazing abundance of foods, including those that, up until now, were only available in season. So stock up! If you're a bread baker, you'll probably want to have a variety of flours, seeds, and dried fruits on hand. Likewise, the pantries of adventurous cooks may hold a fascinating collection of exotic sauces, chutneys, and relishes. Just be sure to buy no more than you can use in a reasonable amount of time.

THE CARE AND KEEPING OF PANTRIES

In Colonial times, food was kept in root cellars and other cool, dark places. Food is no different today—it still keeps best in cool, dry, dark places. Store all edibles as far as possible from stoves, ovens, sunny windows, or other warm spots, and check to make sure there are no heating ducts close enough to raise temperatures near food.

Try to maintain surrounding temperatures below 85 degrees Fahrenheit (75 degrees Fahrenheit is better; 50 degrees Fahrenheit is best). And to keep crackers, cookies, chips, and cereals crisp—and sugars, salt, and baking powder free flowing—keep humidity low in areas where they're stored. Keep cabinets clean to prevent outbreaks of things that scurry.

Refrigerators should be kept frost-free. Check dates on fresh foods, and purchase only what you can use during its peak freshness. Put cold and frozen groceries away first. Use only half a can of tomato paste? Transfer unused portions of food to covered plastic or glass containers. After opening, refrigerate salsa, ketchup, chutney, and sauces. Store ground coffee and coffee beans in the freezer to maintain their freshness longer. And remember, too many cardboard containers will affect the moisture content in the freezer and refrigerator.

Baskets with protectors are ideal for storing bottles and jars because whenever one drips or spills, you'll only need to wash the protector. And the basket makes it easy to see what you've got on hand, without the need to sort through the entire shelf.

Getting Organized

First, situate your foods by function. Store all of your baking ingredients together; salad-making oils and vinegars together, snack stuff with snack stuff, and so on. In the broader scheme, a good rule to follow is "store like with like." Canned beans are grouped with other canned vegetables; packages of spaghetti go with other dried pastas; cereals go in the breakfast foods' section, and so on. Trust us—this not only looks neater, it's more efficient. When you can see at a glance exactly what's on your shelves, you won't overbuy or waste time rummaging around for things.

ORGANIZATION TIP

HERE'S ONE SYSTEM THAT MANY COOKS FIND HANDY
(pictured at left)

TOP SHELF
Lightweight packages of cereal , pastas, rice, crackers, and chips

MIDDLE SHELF
Oils, vinegars, not-too-large packages of flours, sugars, and other dry goods

LOWER SHELF
Canned goods and foods in jars, arranged in front of tall bottles

FLOOR
Heavy items such as canned or bottled beverages and baskets of potatoes and onions

DOOR
(not pictured)
Hang racks for stashing spices and other dry ingredients in small containers

B

A

C

Baskets Are Naturally Neat

Baskets make particularly good organizers because they can be moved around easily; especially those with handles. Experiment with baskets like our Large Berry Basket. With a Bread Woodcrafts Divider, it keeps napkins, and salt and pepper shakers neat and tidy. Or create a snack center with our Serving Tray and its divided protector (Photo A).

Crunched for space? Look for creative ways to make use of every available inch on counters and walls. Our Small Baker's Rack™ (Photo B), makes an excellent breakfast bar stocked with granolas, energy bars, dried fruit, and packets of hot cocoa mix.

Our reader-friendly Book Keeper Basket (Photo C), can house a collection of recipe books. It's pretty enough to keep on the countertop, close at hand. And strong enough to be easily moved, fully loaded, to a spot that's more out of the way.

Recycle, Recycle, Recycle

Have you noticed that, with space in today's kitchen at a premium, we're asking more and more from our pantry areas? Everything from pet food to cleaning supplies to rollerblades somehow lands here by default. But if any nonfood item had a right to claim space here, it would be recyclables. If your family recycles, and we sincerely hope you do, a convenient spot near where recyclables are generated will help keep you in the habit.

We can help with recycling, too. See the photo at right? That's our beautiful Wash Day™ Basket on the left, filled with newspapers. In the center, our Wrought Iron Basket Bin Organizer™ is fitted with a Large Basket Bin on the bottom for old magazines, a Medium Basket Bin in the middle for trash bags and stuff, and on top, a Long Tissue™ Basket that dispenses plastic grocery bags one at a time. The Large Oval Waste Basket on the right is a perfect place for cans. Be sure to use protectors in all your Longaberger recycling baskets—they'll pop right out when it's time to take everything out to the curb for weekly pick-up.

THE WELL-STOCKED PANTRY

Most cooks prefer to cook with fresh ingredients. And most of us prefer to eat meals made with fresh ingredients! But even the extremely conscientious among us sometimes find themselves in a bind, with no time to shop, and expectant faces popping into the kitchen. That's why smart cooks have a variety of foods on hand that keep well, and that can be combined quickly into great-tasting, last-minute meals.

We've put together a list of reliable staples that are good for any cook to consistently keep in the kitchen. Feel free to add to the list, creating one that uniquely reflects your interests and your family's tastes. Quantities are based on a family of four or five.

Oils and Vinegars

A small selection of oils and vinegars can lend infinite diversity to basic recipes, so have on hand at least 1 bottle of each:

Extra-virgin olive oil

Virgin olive oil

Sesame oil

Vegetable oil (or any other unflavored oil)

Walnut oil (store in the refrigerator)

Solid vegetable shortening (for pie pastry—store in the freezer)

Balsamic vinegar

Champagne vinegar

Red wine vinegar (or aged sherry vinegar for a more robust flavor)

Rice wine vinegar

SMART TIP

OLIVE OIL 101

Olive oils possess a range of distinct characteristics, and each can contribute slightly different nuances to a dish. Extra-virgin olive oil is produced from the first cold pressing of the olives. Oils from the second pressing are called "pure" or "virgin" olive oils. Use extra-virgin olive oils whenever possible for seasoning and salads as they have more flavor and character.

Dried Beans/Pastas/Grains

Have on hand 1-pound packages of each:

Black beans (for vegetarian chili)

Lentils

White beans

Bow Tie pasta

Elbow macaroni

Penne pasta

Spaghetti

Couscous (to accompany stews or grilled meats)

Arborio rice (ideal for making risotto)

Regular white rice (good for pilafs and rice salads)

Regular brown rice (a bit more water and cooking time required)

Basmati rice (a little more expensive than ordinary rice, but worth it)

Canned Foods

Have on hand 1 or 2 cans of each:

Whole tomatoes in juice
Diced tomatoes
Tomato juice
Tomato paste
Beef broth
Chicken broth
Anchovies (packed in olive oil)
Tuna fish (albacore)

Condiments

Dijon mustard
Yellow mustard
Ketchup
Fruit chutney
Salsa verde
Family's favorite salsa

Potatoes

Russets (best for baking and French fries)
5 pounds red-skinned potatoes (for salads or boiling)
5 to 10 pounds Idaho and Yukon Gold potatoes
   (best for mashed potatoes)
Heirloom potatoes are now available in some markets. Look for
"fingerlings" to use in place of small red-skinned potatoes.

Onions

Onions will hold 1 to 2 weeks; buy amounts you'll use in that time.

2 pounds red onions
2 pounds white onions
5 or 6 shallots
2 heads fresh garlic (not jarred)

SMART TIP

WHAT'S THE DIFFERENCE BETWEEN CHUTNEY AND SALSA?

*Chutney is generally used as an accompaniment
or sauce for appetizers and main course dishes.
Chutney originated from India, and is best
described as a savory preserve of fruits, vinegars,
sugar, and spices. It is best used with Indian food or
as a condiment for cold sliced meats. Salsas come
from Mexican cuisine and are mixtures of fruits,
herbs, vegetables, and seasonings. They can be hot,
sweet, sour, smooth, crunchy, or a combination.*

SUBSTITUTION TIP

OUT OF UNSWEETENED CHOCOLATE?

Use 3 tablespoons baking cocoa and 1 tablespoon melted unsalted butter for every ounce of unsweetened chocolate called for in your recipe.

Baking Supplies

White, cake, and bread flours stay fresh for 6 months. Be sure to store supplies in airtight containers in a cool, dark place.

Brown sugar
Confectioners' sugar
Sugar (cane sugar caramelizes far better than beet sugar)
White flour
Cake flour
Bread flour
Whole wheat flour (store in the freezer.)
Pure vanilla extract
Baking powder (remains stable for 1 year)
Baking soda (remains stable for 1 year)
Cornstarch (a last-minute thickener for sauces and gravies)

Chocolate

Store chocolate sealed in airtight containers, or tightly wrapped in foil then placed in an airtight plastic bag. Store in a cool, dark place for up to 2 years. It sometimes develops cloudy gray streaks, or "bloom," which will not affect its flavor.

Milk chocolate
Semisweet or bittersweet chocolate (The two can be used to substitute for each other in baking recipes.)
Unsweetened chocolate
White chocolate
Chocolate chips
Baking cocoa and Dutch cocoa (Dutch cocoa works best to give baked desserts a darker appearance. Baking cocoa is best used in hot beverages.)

Nuts

Nuts can turn rancid very quickly. Store them in an airtight container in the refrigerator or freezer. Smell and taste nuts before adding to a batter; if they taste rancid, throw them away. Have on hand 1 pound of each:

Almonds   Pecans   Pine Nuts   Walnuts

Room Temperature Foods

Avocados	Peaches	Plums
Bananas	Pears	Tomatoes

Refrigerator Foods

Fruits (Store in the crisper section):

Assorted apples	Grapes	Limes
Berries	Kiwifruit	Oranges
Grapefruit	Lemons	Pineapples

Vegetables (Store in the crisper section):

Asparagus	Cucumbers	Salad greens
Bell peppers	Green beans	Summer squash
Broccoli	Wax beans	(will hold 5 days)
Carrots	Mushrooms	Zucchini

Dairy:

Yogurt, plain (for fruit smoothies, dips, dressings, or marinades)	Milk	Jack cheese
	Cream	Parmesan cheese
	Sour cream	Swiss cheese
	Cheddar cheese, mild to sharp	Eggs (farm-fresh eggs have the best flavor)
Unsalted butter		

Freezer Foods

Ground beef patties (homemade)	Pastry dough	Ice cream and/or sorbet
Vegetable and meat stocks	Frozen vegetables	Brownies or pound cake
	French fries	Coffee beans or ground coffee (coffee beans last longer)
Bacon	Fruits	
Pizza crust	Fruit juices	

ESSENTIAL SEASONINGS

Fresh herbs and spices are always preferred as dried herbs lose their punch over time. When buying dried herbs, purchase small quantities, and whole leaves or seeds, whenever possible. Check to make sure their containers are kept tightly sealed, and keep them out of light. Herbs and spices in clear glass jars, arranged alphabetically in a cabinet or drawer, are easier to identify and grab when time is short. Label herbs and spices with purchase date; throw them away one year after their purchase.

Essentials

Basil

Cayenne pepper

Chili powder

Chives

Cinnamon (sticks and ground)

Cloves (whole and ground)

Cumin

Dry mustard

Ginger

Nutmeg (purchase whole and grate small amounts as needed)

Oregano

Paprika

Rosemary

Tarragon

Thyme

Whole black peppercorns (try Tellicherry from southern India)

Red pepper flakes

Sea salt (coarse and fine)

Table salt

Extras

Allspice (whole and ground)

Bay leaves

Cardamom pods

Chinese five-spice powder

Coriander

Curry powder

Dill

Garam masala (a blend used in Indian cooking)

Lavender

Mace

Marjoram

Poppy seeds

Saffron

Sage

Savory

Sesame seeds

Szechwan pepper

Turmeric (often used for making mustards and curries)

Wasabi (a Japanese mustard)

White peppercorns

In a word? Tasting. As foods come into contact with other ingredients, change in temperature, or cure over time, their flavors change. That's why it's important to season food as you cook. Taste, season, then taste and re-season again, if necessary. Dumping in seasonings when the recipe is finished will give you different results than if you season throughout the cooking process. And remember, salt has the unique ability to complement and intensify so many flavors. Decrease it in your recipes if you must for health reasons, but try not to eliminate it altogether. And never change salt measurements in baked goods, as it's a critical part of the chemical equation.

Substitutions for Spices

What happens if you're in the middle of a recipe and find yourself out of a key seasoning? Try these easy substitutions.

Allspice	Use cinnamon with a pinch of nutmeg and ground cloves
Basil	Use oregano and thyme in equal portions
Cardamom	Use ginger
Chili powder	Use hot pepper sauce or hot pepper sauce with a pinch of cumin and oregano
Chives	Use green onions
Cinnamon	Use nutmeg plus a pinch of allspice
Cloves	Use allspice, cinnamon, and nutmeg in equal portions
Ginger	Use allspice, cinnamon, mace, and nutmeg in equal portions
Marjoram	Use basil, oregano, savory, and thyme in equal portions
Nutmeg	Use mace
Oregano	Use basil, marjoram, and thyme in equal portions
Red pepper flakes	Use a few drops of hot sauce
Rosemary	Use savory, tarragon, and thyme in equal portions
Saffron	Use a pinch of turmeric (for color only)
Sage	Use marjoram, rosemary, savory, and thyme in equal portions
Thyme	Use basil, marjoram, oregano, and savory in equal portions

EQUIPPED FOR ANYTHING

It's entirely possible to get by in the kitchen with a bowl, a big spoon, a sharp knife, and a saucepan. But why? A sensible assortment of bakeware, cookware, and small appliances can make short work of the tasks that you don't find particularly fun. Leaving you with more time for those tasks that you do.

And since this book is brought to you by Longaberger®, may we just quickly point out that our pottery is made from American vitrified china, which means it resists chipping, cracking, crazing, and dulling over time. It's freezer, microwave, dishwasher, and oven safe, and comes in a variety of classic colors. Looks great with our baskets, too.

Bakeware

1-quart casserole
2-quart casserole
8 × 8-inch baking dish
9 × 13-inch baking dish
5 × 9-inch loaf dish
4-cup soufflé dish
8-cup soufflé dish
8- or 9-inch round baking pans
Muffin pans

Heavy-gauge cookie sheets (one edge bent, the other three sides flat)
Heavy-gauge jelly roll pans (basically a cookie sheet with a rim around all sides)
9-inch diameter pie plate (our Grandma Bonnie's™ Pie Plate is extra deep, with a wide rim to catch juices from warm fruit pies)

Pots and Pans

Roasting pan (at least 3 inches deep, with handles to make it easy to remove from the oven)
Broiling pan
V-shaped roasting rack (for holding roasting meats out of their juices)
2-, 4-, and 6-quart saucepans with lids (stainless or anodized stainless steel)
10- or 12-quart stockpot with lid (Choose lightweight aluminum for boiling pasta and stainless for making stocks. Use the lid to speed up boiling.)
10- or 12-inch cast-iron skillet (for browning and frying meat, or for baking corn bread. When cleaning cast-iron skillets, allow the skillet to cool, then wash with hot water, rinse well, and return the skillet to heat to dry. Rub a small amount of vegetable oil on the skillet's surface between uses to keep it well seasoned.)
6- or 8-inch nonstick skillet
12- or 14-inch nonstick skillet

Bowls

Well-equipped kitchens boast an assortment of different-sized bowls. One set of Longaberger Pottery® bowls is perfect. They're nonreactive to acids so flavors aren't affected. Pottery bowls are practical because food can be prepared in them and then served at the table with style.

THE APPLIANCE GARAGE

Pause here to evaluate all the small appliances that you own. Those that you use daily, or at least weekly, get a place of honor on your countertop. Others, like blenders and mixers, keep close at hand behind cabinet doors. Those that come out less than twice a year, say tube pans and waffle irons, stash elsewhere (don't dismiss under the bed).

Essential

Toaster

Blender (for fruit drinks and puréed soups)

Food processor (chops, slices, helps prepare doughs)

Electric hand mixer (purées vegetables and sauces, mixes vinaigrettes)

Stand mixer

Microwave oven (reheats leftovers, steams vegetables, melts chocolate)

Coffee maker

Nice to Have

Deep fryer

Waffle iron

Ice cream maker

Rice cooker

Coffee grinder

Spice grinder (for grinding your own blends)

Charcoal kettle grill

Copper pans (they heat evenly and quickly)

4- or 6-quart Dutch oven (ridged-bottom, cast-iron)

Grill pan (for in-house grilling)

French tart pans (with removable bottoms)

Springform pans (for cheesecakes)

Tube pan (for angel food cakes)

Parchment paper (for lining cookie sheets and cake pans)

Pastry bags (for decorating)

Cookie cutters

Small ice cream scoop (for portioning cookie dough)

Meat cleaver

Food mill (purées soup, salads, sauces, and baby foods)

Scale (for precise measurements)

Gadgets and Gear

Whenever possible, select the best tools you can find and afford. Quite often quality makes a big difference. And if you're investing your time in cooking, your time will be best spent with equipment that's a pleasure to use.

Knives

Reread the sentence above about investing in quality, because good knives are a sizable investment. Quality knives, though, can eliminate the need for many silly kitchen gadgets. And if your knives are cared for properly, they can last several lifetimes.

Knives should be given a few quick strokes on the sharpening steel after several uses. Wash them by hand and dry them quickly; don't leave them to soak. Use your kitchen knives only for kitchen tasks—no prying open jars or tightening screws. And store them in a knife block where they're easily accessible, not tossed in a drawer where other utensils can nick their edges.

For the average kitchen, full-tang knives forged from high-carbon stainless steel are best. (The tang is the portion of the knife blade that is sunk into the handle.) Cheaper, carbon-steel knives need more care, although they do keep a sharp edge longer than stainless steel.

Basic Knives

8- or 10-inch chef knife (for basic cutting, slicing, chopping)

12-inch slicing knife (for slicing meats and fish)

8- or 10-inch bread knife (for cutting bread and tomatoes; doesn't need sharpening)

2- or 3-inch paring knife (for peeling vegetables and fruits)

1 sharpening steel

1 pair of well-made kitchen shears (for cutting poultry, trimming meat, cutting soft breads, snipping herbs)

1 knife block (for storing knives, on the countertop or in a drawer)

Cutting Boards

At least one cutting board should be at least 14 × 16 inches. Proper chopping requires a large area.

Choose wood or plastic cutting boards.

Keep them washed and sanitized.

Designate one board exclusively for cutting meats to avoid bacteria transfers.

Measuring Tools

1 or 2 sets of measuring spoons (1 tablespoon, 1/2 tablespoon, 1 teaspoon, 3/4 teaspoon, 1/2 teaspoon, 1/4 teaspoon, 1/8 teaspoon)

1 set of dry measuring cups (1 cup, 3/4 cup, 1/3 cup, 1/2 cup, 1/4 cup)

1 (2-cup) liquid measuring cup

1 (6-cup) liquid measuring cup

(When measuring liquids, check amounts at eye level.)

Utensils

Bottle opener

Can opener (Buy the best and keep it out of the dishwasher. If the handle becomes tight, spritz the gears with vegetable cooking spray.)

Cork screw

Lemon reamer (Cut lemons into halves; press reamer in to release juice.)

Vegetable peeler (Throw away when the blade becomes dull.)

Pastry brushes (Buy at least 2: One to be used exclusively for brushing oil and sauces onto meat; the other to be used exclusively for brushing butter or egg glazes onto pastry dough.)

Long-handled fork (for piercing and turning foods)

Funnel (for transferring liquids to small-mouthed containers)

Ladles (assorted sizes)

Metal spatula (for removing cookies from cookie sheets)

2 flexible rubber spatulas (for scraping bowls, folding batters)

Mixing spoons (an assortment of small, medium, and large spoons)

Wooden spoons (3 or 4 are ideal. Keep them out of the dishwasher.)

Tongs (1 small and 1 large, for turning and lifting food)

Wire whisks (One small and lightweight for dressings, syrups, and marinades. One balloon whisk for whipping cream and meringues.)

Gadgets and Gear

Large aluminum colander (for draining pasta and cooked rice)

3-inch sieve (for dusting confectioners' sugar or straining small quantities)

8-inch sieve (for straining stocks, soups, and sauces)

Box grater (for grating cheese or making bread crumbs)

Pastry blender (for cutting unsalted butter into flour for pastry dough)

Peppermill (for the freshest, most pungent pepper flavor)

Rolling pin

Meat thermometer

Timer

Salad spinner (to dry just-washed salad greens and herbs)

Kitchen towels (an assortment of sizes)

Pot holders (an assortment of sizes)

BEFORE

AFTER

ORGANIZATION TIP
DECLUTTERING DRAWERS

Almost every Longaberger Basket® was designed to hold a "protector," a thin plastic sheath that lines and protects the inside of the basket. Because they come in so many shapes and sizes, they're also perfect for organizing kitchen drawers. See photo above.

SPECIALS OF THE DAY

After cooking meals for a family of twelve for almost eighty years, even Grandma Bonnie Longaberger admits to sometimes being stumped for new menu ideas. Like her, most of us are easily overwhelmed by the many factors to consider: Time of day? Casual or impressive? What's in the freezer? What's on sale? Who likes what? How many are coming? The trick is to start with the entrée. Then add side dishes that contrast with the main dish in color, texture, taste, and temperature. Sound tricky? Practice with the prearranged menus we've provided, composed mostly of recipes found in this book.

Light Suppers

Option I
Mixed salad greens with Asian
    Ginger Lime Dressing, page 29
Chicken Satay with Peanut Sauce
    (entrée portions), page 36
Rice Pilaf, page 134
Broccoli Sauté (use sesame oil),
    page 114
Sliced Summer Melon in Lime
    Syrup, page 178

Option II
Grilled Salmon with Roasted
    Red Pepper Sauce, page 76
Jicama Slaw, page 116
Steamed Asparagus
Berry Granita, page 182

Vegetarian

Option I
Wedge of iceberg with Balsamic
    Vinaigrette, page 29
Tomato Sauce with Spaghetti, page 128
Pesto Garlic Bread, page 129
Classic Cheesecake, page 156

Option II
Black Bean Soup (without the ham),
    page 56
Green Salad with Garlic Lemon
    Dressing, page 29
Cheese Biscuits, page 142
Blueberry Crisp with Vanilla Bean Ice
    Cream, pages 176 and 180

Option III
Tomato Carrot Cilantro Soup, page 52
Spanish Potato Omelet, page 100
Mixed salad greens with Basic
    Vinaigrette, page 28
Fresh Apricot Deep-Dish Pie, page 170

SHALL WE START?

Here in Central Ohio, we remember when a party wasn't a party without a big bowl of potato chips and onion dip. These days, the word "appetizer" has a whole new meaning, and this selection of recipes reflects that. Today, you might choose one of our soups or salads as a starter for a formal dinner. Other times, you'll find that the same soup or salad becomes the star of a light, casual meal. Many of the recipes, like our Quesadillas, make fun, substantial snacks. Still other times, you'll want to mix and match several of your favorites to create an entire menu. Try starting with the fresh, cool Cucumber Mint Soup, for instance. Follow with a fresh salad with Asian Ginger Lime Dressing, paired with Chicken Satay with Peanut Sauce. The trick to making it all work? The freshest, best-quality ingredients you can find. And a big splash of creativity.

IS IT A SALAD DAY?

IS IT A SALAD DAY? If you're a big fan of tossed greens, you're not the first. The word "salad" has been traced as far back as the ancient Romans. Their word for it literally meant "to salt," because of the importance salt has as an ingredient in salad dressings. Eventually the French coined the word "salade." The first recorded use of the word "salade" can be found in a recipe book composed before 1399!

Fresh greens tossed with an excellent vinaigrette make a lovely salad starter to almost any brunch, lunch or dinner. On the next few pages you'll find a simple vinaigrette, plus a few easy variations to get you started creating your own famous blend. Once you get the hang of it, you'll find that this lively little dressing perks up the flavors of more dishes than salads, so make plenty and keep it on hand.

MIX AND MATCH A DIFFERENT SALAD DAILY

Toss any of these tastemakers with mixed greens, or serve the "combination of the day" simply arranged on a bed of crisp lettuce:

Plain or flavored croutons
Grated Parmesan or asiago cheese
Crumbled bleu cheese
Warm goat cheese
Diced New York white Cheddar cheese
Sliced pears, apples, grapes, berries
Dried fruit
Toasted pecans
Toasted pine nuts

Spicy walnuts
Grilled or roasted meats
Smoked fish
Marinated artichokes
Marinated mushrooms
Pitted olives
Chopped fresh vegetables
Grilled vegetables

CHOOSING AND CLEANING SALAD GREENS

If you've visited any produce department lately, you know that iceberg lettuce is no longer the only option. Take advantage of the variety offered, and remember that color equals nutrients. Try boldly flavored greens like arugula, watercress, or radicchio—alone, or mingled with milder salad greens. Always choose salad greens that are crisp and blemish-free.

To clean greens, simply trim and discard discolored or tough outer leaves. Place remaining greens in a bowl or sink filled with cold water and gently swish them around. Carefully lift the greens from the water and place in a bowl or colander. Repeat the process until the rinse water is clear and free of dirt. Then, because salad dressing won't cling to wet leaves, spin salad greens dry in a salad spinner.

Remove greens and gently roll them up in paper towels. Place in a plastic bag poked with holes and store in the crisper drawer of your refrigerator for up to one week.

BASIC VINAIGRETTE

BASIC VINAIGRETTE

From the
Longaberger
Pantry

1/4   cup red wine vinegar
2   teaspoons Dijon mustard
1   shallot, minced
    Salt and freshly cracked pepper to taste
3/4   cup extra-virgin olive oil

Combine the red wine vinegar, Dijon mustard, shallot, salt and pepper in a bowl and mix well with a whisk. Add the olive oil a small amount at a time, whisking constantly until blended. Adjust the seasonings to taste.

Makes 1 cup

Preparing vinaigrette is incredibly easy, and once you've tasted your own, you'll never go back to bottled. Go ahead and experiment with different vinegars, oils, herbs, mustards, whatever. Just remember the basic proportions—one part acid to three parts oil—and you can't go wrong.

V A R I A T I O N S

For **Vinaigrette Chicken,** pour Basic Vinaigrette over chicken in a plastic food storage bag and seal. Marinate in the refrigerator for 30 minutes to 24 hours. Prepare the chicken by grilling or broiling. The marinade will make the chicken tasty and tender.

For **Zesty Bread,** cut a loaf of French bread into slices and place on a baking sheet. Drizzle Basic Vinaigrette over the bread and sprinkle with Parmesan cheese. Bake at 350 degrees for 8 to 10 minutes or until toasted and golden brown.

For **Grilled Vegetables,** cut vegetables as you like, keeping in mind the more cut surface the better. Brush a grill rack with some vegetable oil to prevent the vegetables from sticking. Brush some of the Basic Vinaigrette on the vegetables and place on the prepared grill rack. Grill the vegetables on both sides and as you remove them from the grill, brush again with Basic Vinaigrette.

For **Vinaigrette Shrimp,** drizzle hot grilled shrimp or scallops with Basic Vinaigrette and serve atop cooked pasta.

For **Reduced-Fat Vinaigrette,** reduce the amount of olive oil to 1/4 cup and add 1/4 cup chicken broth and 1/2 cup nonfat plain yogurt. Reduce the red wine vinegar to 2 tablespoons and add 2 tablespoons fresh lemon juice.

ASIAN GINGER LIME DRESSING

From the
Longaberger
Pantry

1/4 cup lime juice	1 shallot, minced
2 teaspoons rice wine vinegar	2 tablespoons toasted sesame seeds
2 teaspoons soy sauce	Salt and pepper
5 teaspoons Dijon mustard	to taste
	1/2 cup canola oil
2 tablespoons grated gingerroot	1/4 cup sesame oil

Combine all the ingredients in a bowl and mix well. This dressing is great splashed over a grilled chicken and watercress salad.

BALSAMIC VINAIGRETTE

From the
Longaberger
Pantry

1/4 cup balsamic vinegar	1 teaspoon minced thyme
2 teaspoons Dijon mustard	1/2 teaspoon minced marjoram
1 shallot, minced	
1 tablespoon chopped parsley	Salt and pepper to taste
4 teaspoons minced garlic	3/4 cup extra-virgin olive oil

Combine all the ingredients in a bowl and mix well. Serve over wedges of iceberg lettuce sprinkled with bleu cheese and crisp, crumbled bacon.

GARLIC LEMON DRESSING

From the
Longaberger
Pantry

1/4 cup lemon juice	1 garlic clove, minced
4 teaspoons Dijon mustard	
1 shallot, minced	Salt and pepper to taste
2 tablespoons chopped fresh chives	3/4 cup extra-virgin olive oil

Combine all the ingredients in a bowl and mix well. Serve over chilled asparagus or any chilled vegetable you prefer.

GOLF CLUB HOUSE SALAD

Tami Longaberger, President and CEO of The Longaberger® Company, was so impressed with this elegant salad, created by our own Executive Chef at the Longaberger Golf Club® that she suggested it become the house salad. It just might become your house salad, too.

From the Longaberger Pantry

GOLF CLUB HOUSE SALAD

1	cup red raspberries
1	cup balsamic vinegar or red wine vinegar
1/2	cup walnut oil or salad oil
1/8	teaspoon kosher salt
1/8	teaspoon pepper
1 1/2	pounds mixed baby greens
2	cups red raspberries
2	cups blueberries
1	cup crumbled feta cheese
1	cup pine nuts, walnut halves or pecan halves

Combine 1 cup raspberries, balsamic vinegar, walnut oil, kosher salt and pepper in a food processor container. Process at low speed until blended. Divide the greens between 4 salad bowls. Sprinkle each portion evenly with 2 cups raspberries, blueberries, feta cheese and pine nuts. Drizzle with the vinaigrette. Have fun spicing up this vinaigrette with your favorite fresh herbs. Maybe thyme and basil?

Serves 4

Feed the Birds

Fun in the kitchen needn't be limited to cooking meals. Why not maximize precious family time by supervising a project like this one for a simple bird feeder? Older kids can do the melting over low heat; younger children can stir and pack the mixture into containers. When it's finished, everyone's invited to the bird buffet! Tami Longaberger, a long-time bird lover, shared the how-to's for this fun feast for our feathered friends. "I like to add dried currants, cranberries, or raisins to this, too," she says. "That really brings them in!"

Wild Bird Suet Cake

1	cup crunchy peanut butter
1	cup lard
1	cup flour
2	cups quick-cooking oats
2	cups cornmeal
1/3	cup sugar

Melt the peanut butter and lard in a saucepan over low heat. Stir in other ingredients. Divide the mixture among shallow rectangular containers (Tami's family uses recycled tofu containers) and place in the freezer; freeze until firm. Pop out of containers and hang outside in recycled onion bags or other suitable holders. Enjoy the party!

Caesar Salad

This is a simple, classic Caesar dressing. If you choose to omit the anchovies, you may need to adjust the saltiness with a little more grated Parmesan cheese or an extra sprinkle of salt. This salad also tops Caesar Burgers (pages 92 and 93).

CAESAR SALAD		From the Longaberger Pantry
3	whole anchovy fillets	
1	egg	
2	garlic cloves	
3	tablespoons grated Parmesan cheese	
3	tablespoons lemon juice	
3/4	teaspoon salt	
1/4	teaspoon pepper	
1/2	cup olive oil	
2	heads romaine	
1	(6-ounce) package garlic- and butter-flavored croutons	
1	cup shredded Parmesan cheese, or to taste	

Process the anchovies, egg, garlic, Parmesan cheese, lemon juice, salt and pepper in a blender or food processor until blended. Add the olive oil in a fine stream, processing constantly until blended. Tear the romaine into bite-size pieces and place in a salad bowl. (Our Cake Basket with protector or Large Mixing Bowl are perfect options.) Add the croutons and shredded Parmesan cheese and toss to mix. Add the dressing and toss to coat. Serve immediately.

Serves 4

VARIATIONS

Marinated grilled shrimp or chicken breast slices turn this Caesar Salad into a main course. Pressed for time? Pick up a roasted chicken at the grocery store. Shred the chicken, discarding the skin and bones. Add to the Caesar Salad, toss to mix and serve.

Want to improve on store-bought croutons? Make your own *Homemade Crouton Wedges.* Cut a loaf of French bread into halves lengthwise. Cut each half at an angle at 2-inch intervals. Brush with olive oil. Bake at 350 degrees for 8 to 10 minutes or until toasted and golden brown. Remove from the oven. Cut a head of garlic in half. Rub each crouton with the cut side of the garlic head. Sprinkle with fine sea salt. Serve while warm or at room temperature.

HEALTHY TIP

LOW-CALORIE CAESAR DRESSING

Eliminate the egg. Substitute 1/2 cup nonfat sour cream for the olive oil; add 2 to 3 tablespoons skim milk and 1 tablespoon Worcestershire sauce. Follow the directions (above right).

SERVING TIP

A DIFFERENT ARRANGEMENT

*This Caesar Salad requires a knife, but it's no less delicious. Arrange
six to eight leaves of romaine on a salad plate. Drizzle the whole leaves with
dressing and top with shreds of fresh Parmesan cheese. Garnish the salad with
Homemade Crouton Wedges (previous page) and lemon wedges.*

Rachel's Fruity Spinach Salad

Rachel Longaberger, President of The Longaberger Foundation, shares this recipe for one of her favorite salads, along with a suggested variation. She says this salad is easy enough to make for the family, fancy enough for company, pretty on the plate, and healthy, too!

RACHEL'S FRUITY SPINACH SALAD

From the Longaberger Pantry

6	cups torn spinach leaves
1	cup sliced strawberries
1/2	cup blueberries
1	(11-ounce) can mandarin oranges, drained
1/2	cup poppy seed salad dressing
1	tablespoon lemon juice
1	teaspoon sugar (optional)

Combine the spinach leaves, strawberries, blueberries and mandarin oranges in a salad bowl and toss to mix. Mix the poppy seed dressing, lemon juice and sugar in a bowl or place in a shaker and shake to mix well. Drizzle the dressing over the salad and toss to coat. Rachel has also used blackberries or sliced kiwifruit as substitutions for, or in addition to, the fruits used above. Feel free to toss in your family's favorites.

Serves 4

CHICKEN SATAY WITH PEANUT SAUCE

These Thai-style kabobs are perfect to serve at a party, especially when they're presented on our pottery Divided Relish Plate filled with garnishes of sprinkled chopped peanuts, wedges of lime, and cilantro sprigs. For a touch more intensity, add as many chopped serrano chiles to the dipping sauce as you dare. This can also be served as the main course with rice pilaf. Hurray for satay!

CHICKEN SATAY WITH PEANUT SAUCE *From the Longaberger Pantry*

6	boneless skinless chicken breasts	1	tablespoon grated fresh gingerroot
1	tablespoon vegetable oil	1	cup chicken broth
1	tablespoon soy sauce	2	tablespoons soy sauce
1	tablespoon honey	2	tablespoons vinegar
1	tablespoon minced garlic	1	teaspoon sesame oil
		1/3	cup peanut butter

Cut the chicken into strips. Mix the vegetable oil, 1 tablespoon soy sauce, honey, garlic and ginger in a medium bowl. Add the chicken and mix until coated. Thread the chicken onto soaked wooden skewers and place on a grill rack. Grill for 10 minutes or until the juices run clear, turning frequently. Bring the broth, 2 tablespoons soy sauce, vinegar and sesame oil to a simmer in a small saucepan. Add the peanut butter and stir until well blended. Arrange the chicken on skewers on a platter lined with Boston lettuce leaves, julienned carrots and daikon (Asian radishes). Serve with the hot peanut sauce for dipping.

Makes 18 to 24 skewers

VARIATION

For **Beef Satay,** substitute strips of flank steak or beef tenderloin for the chicken. Follow the directions above and grill to the desired degree of doneness. Serve with the Peanut Sauce.

DO-AHEAD TIP
MARINATE AND ASSEMBLE

Marinate the chicken up to a day ahead for extra flavor and tenderness. Assemble the chicken on skewers and refrigerate for 6 to 8 hours in advance. To keep the skewers from burning on the grill, don't forget to soak them in water for 15 minutes.

SERVING TIP

WHAT GOES WITH SATAY?

A speedy **Murinated Cucumber Salad** *makes a cool accompaniment
to satay, especially if you like yours fiery. To make the salad, wash the cucumber.
Cut into thin slices into a salad bowl. Mix 1/4 cup white vinegar, 1/4 cup water,
1 tablespoon sugar, 1 teaspoon salt and 1/4 teaspoon red pepper flakes in a bowl. Pour
over the cucumber. Marinate, covered, in the refrigerator for at least 30 minutes.
Serve the Peanut Sauce in a Custard Cup placed in the center of our Divided Relish
Plate. For dramatic height on a buffet, try inverting our Wrought Iron Pedestal
Stand and place the Divided Relish Plate on top (pictured above).*

ARTICHOKE DIP WITH CRISPY TOASTED PITA CHIPS

We've never met anyone who didn't fall all over themselves getting to this decadent dip. Serve it hot and bubbly, right out of the oven, with thin slices of French bread, bagel chips, water crackers, or our Crispy Toasted Pita Chips (facing page). Ten minutes before the dip is done, pop our Bread Brick into the oven. Serve the dip and its accompaniments in our Bread Basket, with the brick tucked inside to keep everything toasty warm.

ARTICHOKE DIP	From the Longaberger Pantry
8	ounces cream cheese, softened, cut into cubes
1	cup mayonnaise
1	cup sour cream
1	cup grated Parmesan cheese
1	(14-ounce) can artichoke hearts, chopped
1	garlic clove, pressed
1	teaspoon dill
1/8	teaspoon salt
	Crispy Toasted Pita Chips (facing page)

Combine the cream cheese, mayonnaise, sour cream, Parmesan cheese, artichoke hearts, garlic, dill and salt in a food processor container. Process for 1 to 2 minutes or until blended. Spoon into an oiled baking dish. Bake at 375 degrees for 45 to 60 minutes or until the top is golden brown. For best results, use regular, not reduced-fat, mayonnaise or sour cream. Serve warm with Crispy Toasted Pita Chips.
Serves 6 to 8

V A R I A T I O N

If you have a few extra minutes before the guests gather, try *Wild Mushroom Dip.* Substitute 2 pounds wild mushrooms, chopped, for the artichokes. Sauté the mushrooms with 2 tablespoons chopped shallots in 2 tablespoons butter in a skillet until golden brown and all of the liquid evaporates. Let stand until cool. Process the remaining ingredients as directed above. Fold in the mushrooms and bake as directed.

CRISPY TOASTED PITA CHIPS

From the
Longaberger
Pantry

1	large garlic clove, minced
1/8	teaspoon salt
10	tablespoons (1 1/4 sticks) unsalted butter, softened
2	tablespoons minced fresh parsley leaves
1	teaspoon fresh lemon juice
	Salt and pepper to taste
8	miniature pita pockets, cut horizontally into halves

Mash the garlic and 1/8 teaspoon salt in a bowl to form a paste. Cream the butter, garlic paste, parsley and lemon juice in a mixing bowl. Season with salt and pepper to taste. Let stand, covered, for 1 hour. Spread each pita half with some of the butter mixture. Arrange in a single layer on baking sheets. Bake at 400 degrees on the highest oven rack for 5 to 8 minutes or until light brown and crisp. You may prepare Crispy Toasted Pita Chips a day in advance and store in a sealable food storage bag, or prepare up to 2 weeks in advance and freeze. Thaw for several hours before using.

Makes 16 chips

BRUSCHETTA

From the Italian word meaning "roasted over coals," bruschetta is a thick slice of grilled bread with a light topping that's sometimes as simple as fruity green olive oil, fresh garlic, and sea salt. One or two slices make a sophisticated snack; a few more might be served with a salad for a light lunch. Tinier versions of bruschetta called "crostini," or "little toasts," are traditionally served as appetizers. Buono Appetito!

BRUSCHETTA		From the Longaberger Pantry
1 3/4	pounds fresh plum tomatoes (about 12 to 14 tomatoes)	
2	tablespoons minced garlic	
1	cup coarsely chopped fresh basil	
1	teaspoon balsamic vinegar	
1/3	cup olive oil	
	Salt and coarsely ground pepper to taste	
8	slices peasant bread	
1	garlic clove, cut into halves	
1/4	cup olive oil	

Chop the tomatoes into 1/4-inch pieces. Toss with 2 tablespoons garlic in a bowl. Add the basil, vinegar, 1/3 cup olive oil, salt and pepper and mix well. Let stand at room temperature for at least 15 minutes. Rub the bread with the cut sides of the garlic halves and brush with 1/4 cup olive oil. Place on a grill rack. Grill for 5 to 8 minutes or until toasted. Arrange the bread on a serving plate and top with the tomato mixture. Serve immediately.

Makes 8 slices

V A R I A T I O N S

For *White Bean Rosemary Bruschetta,* substitute 2 cups cooked white beans for the tomatoes and substitute 1 tablespoon chopped fresh rosemary and 1/2 cup chopped Italian parsley for the basil.

For *Bruschetta with Wild Mushrooms and Greens,* substitute 1 pound wild mushrooms, chopped and sautéed, and 1 pound kale or spinach, chopped and sautéed, for the tomatoes. Wrap the sautéed kale or spinach in a tea towel and squeeze to remove the excess liquid. Combine with the mushrooms in a bowl and mix well. Follow the directions above, sprinkling with shredded pecorino cheese before serving.

For *Black Olive Bruschetta,* substitute 1 cup slivered pitted olives (Sicilian, kalamata or your favorite kind) for the tomatoes. Substitute chopped fresh Italian parsley for 1/2 cup of the basil.

Shrimp and Mango Salsa in Wonton Cups

The word salsa means "sauce" in both Italian and Spanish, but it's also the name of a sassy Latino dance, and dance is just what this salsa will make your taste buds do! A fresh, chunky salsa that's both mellow and tart—the fresh mango gives it the surprising punch.

	SHRIMP AND MANGO SALSA	From the Longaberger Pantry
24	small wonton wrappers	
	Olive oil or garlic olive oil for brushing	
1	pound (30- to 40-count) shrimp, cooked, peeled, deveined	
1	ripe medium mango, peeled, pitted, chopped	
2	to 3 garlic cloves, minced	
1	cup packed fresh basil leaves, minced	
1/4	cup packed fresh mint leaves, minced	
3/4	cup extra-virgin olive oil	
2	tablespoons lime juice	
	Fresh lemon juice to taste	
	Salt and ground white pepper to taste	

Spray miniature muffin cups with nonstick cooking spray. Press 1 wrapper into each cup and brush lightly with olive oil. Bake at 350 degrees for 7 to 10 minutes or until crisp. Remove from the muffin cups.

Reserve 12 of the shrimp for garnish. Chop the remaining shrimp. Combine the chopped shrimp, mango, garlic, basil, mint, olive oil, lime juice, lemon juice, salt and white pepper in a bowl and mix gently. Adjust the seasonings. Spoon into wonton cups. Cut the reserved shrimp into halves lengthwise. Garnish the top of each with a shrimp half.

Makes 24 wonton cups

VARIATIONS

For *Hot and Spicy Crab Meat and Mango Salsa,* substitute 8 ounces lump crab meat for the shrimp and add 2 tablespoons chopped red onion and 1 teaspoon chopped jalapeño chiles.

For *Chicken and Black Bean Salsa,* substitute 2 chicken breasts, cooked and chopped, for the shrimp; substitute 1/2 cup each roasted corn kernels and black beans for the mango; substitute fresh cilantro for the basil; and substitute fresh Italian parsley for the mint.

TERRACE CAFÉ™
PORTOBELLO MUSHROOMS

This is one of the appetizers served at the Terrace Café™ at Longaberger Homestead® near our company headquarters in Newark, Ohio. Longaberger Homestead is a wonderful place for the whole family to enjoy, with unique shops, restaurants, live entertainment, special celebrations, and so much more. If you can't visit soon, console yourself by making these rich, aromatic mushrooms instead!

TERRACE CAFÉ™ PORTOBELLOS	From the Longaberger Pantry
1/3 cup lemon juice	
1 cup olive oil	
4 (5-inch) portobello mushrooms	
1/2 cup shredded smoked provolone cheese	
2 tablespoons heavy cream, warmed	
1 Roma tomato, chopped	
1 tablespoon chopped fresh parsley	

Mix the lemon juice and olive oil in a small bowl. Pour over the mushrooms in a bowl. Marinate, covered, in the refrigerator for 8 to 12 hours. Drain the mushrooms, discarding the marinade. Pat the mushrooms dry with paper towels. Place the mushrooms top side up on a baking sheet. Bake at 450 degrees for 6 minutes, turning halfway through the baking time. Sprinkle with the cheese. Bake for 2 minutes longer. Place in a warm serving dish. Drizzle the cream over the mushrooms. Cover with the tomato. Sprinkle with parsley. Cut each portobello mushroom into quarters and serve with warm French bread.

Makes 16 mushroom quarters

V A R I A T I O N

For *Portobello, Beet Greens and Fontina Panini,* arrange the marinated and baked portobello mushrooms on thick slices of lightly toasted peasant bread. Add some sautéed chopped beet greens and substitute Italian fontina cheese for the smoked provolone cheese. Sprinkle with chopped tomatoes, some chopped basil and sliced roasted red bell pepper. Top with a second slice of bread.

SMART TIP
WHAT IS PANINI?

Panini is the plural form of the Italian word panino, which means roll, biscuit, or sandwich.

Quesadillas

Gooey melted cheese is the most common component of these tasty tortilla treats, but you don't have to stop there. Start with the familiar quesadilla recipe, then try some of the more adventurous variations below. Once you've tried them all, try them all again—this time using corn tortillas.

VARIATIONS

To punch up the flavor of quesadillas, try adding a few black beans and roasted corn kernels into each tortilla before folding and cooking. Or maybe some cooked and shredded chicken seasoned with lime and topped with a scattering of white Cheddar cheese.

Quesadillas for dessert? You bet! Substitute apple butter for the salsa, Brie for the cheese, and chopped walnuts for the chiles and tomatoes.

QUESADILLAS

From the Longaberger Pantry

1	cup shredded Monterey Jack cheese with jalapeño chiles
1/2	cup shredded Cheddar cheese
1/2	cup salsa
4	flour tortillas
1/2	cup finely chopped tomato
1/4	cup chopped chiles
	Vegetable oil for brushing
	Fresh Guacamole (below)
	Salsa Buena (facing page)
	Sour cream

Mix the Monterey Jack cheese and Cheddar cheese in a bowl. Spread 2 tablespoons salsa over half of each tortilla. Sprinkle each with 2 tablespoons tomatoes and 1 tablespoon chiles. Sprinkle with the cheese mixture. Fold over each tortilla. Brush both sides of the folded tortillas with oil. Place in a heated large nonstick skillet. Cook over medium heat for 3 to 4 minutes on each side. Cut each tortilla into 3 or 4 triangles. Serve with Fresh Guacamole, Salsa Buena and sour cream.

Serves 4

FRESH GUACAMOLE

From the Longaberger Pantry

3	ripe avocados
1/2	small onion, finely chopped
1	garlic clove, minced
1/8	teaspoon chopped fresh jalapeño chile
1	tablespoon lime juice
1/8	teaspoon hot pepper sauce
	Salt and pepper to taste

Mash the avocados coarsely in a medium bowl. Stir in the onion, garlic, chile, lime juice and hot pepper sauce. Season with salt and pepper. Chill, covered, until ready to serve.

Makes 2 cups

SALSA BUENA

From the
Longaberger
Pantry

2	tomatoes, peeled, seeded, coarsely chopped
1/2	green bell pepper, finely chopped
1/4	red bell pepper, finely chopped
1/4	red onion, finely chopped
1	large garlic clove, minced
2	tablespoons olive oil
2	tablespoons fresh lime juice
1	tablespoon white wine vinegar
1	tablespoon chopped fresh basil
1/4	teaspoon oregano
	Salt and pepper to taste

Combine the tomatoes, bell peppers, onion, garlic, olive oil, lime juice, vinegar, basil and oregano in a bowl and mix well. Season with salt and pepper. Chill, covered, for 2 hours.

Makes 3 1/2 cups

CRAB CAKES WITH SPICY RÉMOULADE SAUCE

These are best if made with fresh crab meat, and do allow time to chill the cakes before frying; they'll hold together much better as they cook. We also like these crab cakes served as a main course. Figure four per seafood lover.

CRAB CAKES			From the Longaberger Pantry
1	pound lump crab meat	1	teaspoon dry mustard
1	cup soft bread crumbs		Tabasco sauce to taste
1	egg, lightly beaten		Vegetable oil for frying
1/4	cup mayonnaise		Lemon slices
2	tablespoons minced fresh parsley		Spicy Rémoulade Sauce (below)
			Capers

Mix the crab meat and bread crumbs gently in a bowl. Combine the egg, mayonnaise, parsley, dry mustard and Tabasco sauce in a bowl and mix well. Add to the crab meat mixture and mix gently. Shape into 12 patties. Chill, wrapped in plastic wrap, for 30 minutes. Heat 1/4 inch oil in a skillet to 350 degrees. Fry the crab cakes for 3 minutes on each side or until golden brown. Drain on paper towels. Arrange on a serving plate. Garnish with lemon slices. Top with Spicy Rémoulade Sauce and capers.

    Makes 12 crab cakes

SPICY RÉMOULADE SAUCE			From the Longaberger Pantry
1 1/4	cups mayonnaise	2	tablespoons chopped scallions or green onions
1	hard-cooked egg, finely chopped		
1	tablespoon minced cornichons	1 1/2	teaspoons chopped fresh tarragon
1	tablespoon drained capers	1	teaspoon Dijon mustard
1	garlic clove, minced		Salt and ground pepper to taste
2	tablespoons chopped fresh parsley		

Combine the mayonnaise, egg, cornichons, capers, garlic, parsley, scallions, tarragon and Dijon mustard in a bowl and mix well. Season with salt and pepper. Store in the refrigerator. You may substitute sour gherkins for the cornichons.

    Makes 2 cups

Cucumber Mint Soup

In the heat of the summer, you'll find yourself craving the clean, refreshing flavors of this chilled soup. Toasted sesame seeds add a delicate new dimension. Tote cold soups like this in a thermos for picnics and other outdoor celebrations. But don't wait for summer—it makes a great healthy first course year-round.

CUCUMBER MINT SOUP		From the Longaberger Pantry
1	teaspoon cumin seeds	
3	cups plain yogurt	
2	large cucumbers, peeled, chopped	
3	tablespoons sesame seeds, toasted	
1	tablespoon corn oil	
1/2	teaspoon salt	
2	tablespoons finely chopped fresh mint leaves, or to taste	
1	tablespoon finely chopped fresh cilantro, or to taste	

Toast the cumin seeds in an ungreased medium skillet until brown. Process in a blender to form a powder. Add the yogurt and cucumbers and process until puréed. Stir in the sesame seeds, corn oil, salt, mint and cilantro. Pour into a large bowl. Chill, covered, for 1 hour. Pour into serving containers. Garnish with thinly sliced cucumber and mint leaves. (Note: You may use ground cumin if you don't have time to make it yourself, but remember, fresh-toasted cumin has more flavor and aroma.) Also, try sprinkling the mint and cilantro on top instead of stirring into the soup.

Makes 4 cups

V A R I A T I O N

For *Cool Zucchini Soup,* substitute 3 medium zucchini for the cucumbers and substitute 1/2 bunch fresh watercress for the mint. Garnish the soup with the remaining 1/2 bunch of watercress.

TOMATO BASIL SOUP

This flavorful soup tastes best when made during the height of tomato season, when home gardens are full of the year's freshest, meatiest tomatoes. Other times of the year, we use canned whole or diced tomatoes—their flavor is far superior to that of the pale, watery tomatoes that are otherwise available in markets.

TOMATO BASIL SOUP

1 1/2	cups chopped yellow onions
1	tablespoon minced garlic
2	tablespoons olive oil
2	(15-ounce) cans peeled whole plum tomatoes, or 2 pounds fresh plum tomatoes, peeled
4	cups chicken stock, vegetable stock or water
1	teaspoon dried marjoram
1	teaspoon dried basil
1	teaspoon dried oregano
	Salt and pepper to taste
1/2	cup heavy cream (optional)
1	cup fresh basil, chopped
1/4	cup fresh parsley, chopped
1	cup cooked rice (optional)

Sauté the onions and garlic in the olive oil in a saucepan until transparent. Stir in the tomatoes, stock, dried herbs, salt and pepper. Simmer for 45 minutes. Purée in small batches in a blender and return to the saucepan. (Use caution when puréeing hot soup.) Season with salt and pepper. Stir in the cream, fresh basil and fresh parsley. Divide the rice between 6 soup bowls. Ladle the soup over the rice. Garnish with additional chopped fresh basil or parsley leaves. Serve with Parmesan Cheese Toasts (facing page).

Serves 6

V A R I A T I O N

For *Tomato Carrot Cilantro Soup,* chop 1 pound peeled carrots. Add to the onions and garlic and sauté. Eliminate the marjoram, dried and fresh basil and the oregano. Add 2 teaspoons cumin powder, 1 teaspoon curry powder and 1 bay leaf to the tomatoes and stock. Simmer and remove the bay leaf. Purée as above. Substitute 1/2 cup chopped fresh cilantro for the 1 cup fresh basil.

PARMESAN CHEESE TOASTS

From the
Longaberger
Pantry

1	small loaf quality bread, sliced
1	cup mayonnaise
2	scallions, chopped
1/2	cup grated Parmesan cheese
	Freshly ground pepper to taste

Trim crusts from the bread slices if desired. Cut the bread slices into quarters or bite-size shapes using small cookie cutters. Mix the mayonnaise, scallions, Parmesan cheese and pepper in a small bowl. Spread over the bread slices. Place on a baking sheet. Broil until the cheese mixture turns golden brown and bubbly. Watch carefully to avoid burning.

Makes 20 small slices

BUTTERNUT SQUASH SOUP

Butternut squash, widely grown and available most of the year, is high in vitamin A and fiber. It lends a lovely golden richness to this intriguing soup, but try it also puréed with a dash of cream and a sprinkle of nutmeg to complement roasted game and poultry.

BUTTERNUT SQUASH SOUP			From the Longaberger Pantry
2	medium or large butternut squash	1/2	teaspoon cumin
		1/2	teaspoon coriander
1	teaspoon vegetable oil	1/2	teaspoon cinnamon
		1/4	teaspoon dry mustard
1	large onion, chopped		Cayenne pepper
2	garlic cloves, minced		to taste
2	tablespoons butter	1	(10-ounce) package
4	cups chicken stock		frozen chopped spinach
1	cup orange juice	1/2	cup pumpkin seeds or
1 1/4	teaspoons salt		sunflower seeds,
3/4	teaspoon ginger		toasted

Cut the squash into halves and discard the seeds. Coat the uncut sides with the vegetable oil. Arrange the squash skin side up in a greased baking dish. Add just enough water to cover the bottom of the dish. Bake, covered with foil, at 375 degrees for 1 hour. Scoop the squash pulp into a blender container and process until puréed. Sauté the onion and garlic in the butter in a stockpot. Stir in the puréed squash, chicken stock and orange juice. Sprinkle with the next 7 ingredients. Bring to a boil and reduce the heat. Simmer, covered, for 20 minutes, stirring occasionally. Thaw the spinach and squeeze out the excess moisture. Stir into the soup. Ladle immediately into soup bowls. Sprinkle with the pumpkin seeds.

Makes 5 (1-cup) servings

VARIATIONS

No butternut squash in the pantry? Substitute equal amounts of acorn squash, buttercup squash, or pumpkin instead.

For *Root Vegetable Soup,* cut 2 pounds peeled organic carrots, 2 peeled parsnips and 2 peeled sweet potatoes into 2-inch pieces and place in a baking dish. Roast following the directions above. Purée the roasted vegetables in batches in a food processor. Add the puréed vegetables to the remaining ingredients, adding additional stock if needed for the desired consistency. Garnish each serving with 1 teaspoon sour cream or plain yogurt and a few chopped chives. (Note: Use organic carrots since they are much sweeter and will enhance the overall flavor of the soup.)

SERVING TIP

SOUP WITH GREAT STYLE

Serve soup in warm bowls garnished with créme fraîche or sour cream and a few toasted pumpkin seeds.

For real style, serve your soup in small hollowed-out pumpkins! To make the bowls on the facing page, cut off the upper third of bowl-sized pumpkins with a sharp knife. Scoop out the seeds and, if necessary, some of the pulp. Place the pumpkins, along with their tops, on a baking sheet. Bake at 350 degrees for 18 to 22 minutes or until the pumpkins are slightly tender. Ladle soup into the pumpkins, replace the tops and serve your soup with a flourish.

WHITE BEAN SOUP

Don't let the number of ingredients keep you from making this hearty soup. They all get dumped into one pot, and each contributes to the final, robust flavor. Prepare this soup at least one day in advance to allow the flavors to marry. Got a vegetarian in the house? You can easily adapt this recipe by eliminating the meat and substituting vegetable stock for the chicken stock. We like this soup anytime, but especially on a blustery Ohio day.

PREPARATION TIP
SOAKING BEANS

Dried beans need to soak to rehydrate, which cuts down on cooking time. There are 2 ways to soak the beans. For the quick method, bring the beans to a boil and boil for 2 minutes. Soak, covered, for 1 hour. Drain and follow the recipe (above right).

The second method calls for soaking the beans for 8 to 12 hours and then cooking the beans. Bring the beans to a boil and simmer for 2 hours or until the beans are soft. The cooking time will depend on the type of bean. Always discard the soaking water.

WHITE BEAN SOUP			From the Longaberger Pantry
1 1/2	cups dried small white beans	1	bay leaf
		1	teaspoon pepper
1/4	cup bacon drippings	8	cups chicken broth
1	cup chopped white onion	2	cups chopped red potatoes
1	cup chopped leeks	8	ounces ham hock
2	cups chopped celery	1	cup chopped zucchini
2	carrots, chopped		
2	teaspoons minced garlic	1/2	cup chopped fresh Italian parsley
2	teaspoons fresh thyme		Salt to taste

Rinse and sort the beans. Soak the beans in cold water to cover in a large bowl for 8 to 12 hours; drain. Place the beans in a stockpot and cover with fresh water. Simmer for 2 hours or until tender; drain. Melt the bacon drippings in a heavy stockpot. Add the onion, leeks, celery, carrots and garlic. Sauté for 10 minutes or until tender. Stir in the thyme, bay leaf, pepper and chicken broth. Add the potatoes, ham hock and beans. Bring to a boil and reduce the heat. Simmer for 1 hour. Remove the ham hock to a platter and let stand until cool. Remove the ham from the bone, discarding the bone. Cut the ham into small pieces. Add to the soup. Add the zucchini and parsley. Simmer for 5 to 10 minutes or until tender. Adjust the seasonings, adding salt if needed. Remove the bay leaf. Ladle into soup bowls.

Serves 8

VARIATION

Black beans are rich in both fiber and color. For **Black Bean Soup,** substitute black beans for the white beans and add 1 cup sherry in place of 1 cup of the chicken broth. For a dramatic presentation, ladle soup into bowls and top with sieved hard-cooked egg yolk and chopped egg white. Serve with wedges of warm corn bread.

Gazpacho

The word gazpacho comes from the Arabic word for "soaked bread." Oddly enough, this soup historically has never featured tomatoes, yet tomatoes are what make it "gazpacho" for most Americans. Because tomatoes play such a key role in this recipe, it tastes best when made at the height of tomato-growing season. (Here in the Midwest, that's late summer.) At other times of the year, rely on the reddest, ripest fresh tomatoes you can find.

GAZPACHO	From the Longaberger Pantry
1	cup cubed trimmed French bread
1/3	cup extra-virgin olive oil
1/4	cup red wine vinegar
1	tablespoon chopped garlic
10	to 12 medium red tomatoes, peeled, seeded
1	cucumber, peeled, seeded
1	red bell pepper, seeded, cut into quarters
1	medium red onion, cut into quarters
1/2	cup tomatillo quarters (optional)
	Salt and pepper to taste
1	cup tomato juice (if needed)

Purée the French bread, olive oil, vinegar and garlic in a food processor. Pour into a large bowl. Add the tomatoes, cucumber, bell pepper, onion and tomatillo quarters to the food processor container. Process until puréed. Add to the bread purée and whisk until combined. Season with salt and pepper. Add tomato juice if needed to make of the desired consistency. Chill, covered, for 2 to 3 hours. Ladle into chilled soup bowls. Garnish with diced red or white onion, chopped scallions, toasted croutons and diced tomatoes. You may add a dash of hot sauce and, if the tomatoes lack flavor, add 1 cup tomato juice.

Serves 8

VARIATIONS

For *White Gazpacho,* substitute 2 additional cucumbers for the red tomatoes. Use green bell pepper instead of the red. Use 1/2 cup almond flour instead of the puréed bread mixture.

For *Yellow Tomato Gazpacho,* use yellow tomatoes and bell peppers instead of the red, a white onion instead of the red onion and white wine vinegar in place of the red wine vinegar. Garnish with chopped fresh cilantro.

WHAT'S FOR DINNER?

Psssst. Here's a little secret about main courses: They get all the attention, yet often require the least effort. Especially the recipes you'll find here. We've chosen a variety of economical meats that are decently lean, and balanced them with healthy helpings of poultry and fish. The cooking methods are time-savers, too: grilling, roasting and pan-searing. And don't count on a bevy of extra ingredients to add excitement, because they're not here. Aside from a few bold seasonings, we'll show you how to rely on your entrées' simple succulence and mouth-watering aromas to tempt your family and friends to the table. Most kids don't go for too much fancy stuff anyway. Oh, and we've also included a few recipes for main-dish pastas, like Healthy Turkey Lasagna, for a delectable change of pace.

HOW DO YOU LIKE YOUR CHICKEN?

If you're like the majority of Americans, you like all-white meat best, as in chicken breasts, boned, skinned, and split down the middle. Once considered a special treat reserved for Sunday dinners or special occasions, today's chicken is inexpensive and found in abundance in almost any grocery store. And whether you prefer breast meat to drumsticks, it's all relatively low in fat, cholesterol, and calories. And chicken's mild flavor makes it a natural for taking on seasonings in marinades, dry rubs, and sauces.

One of our favorite ways to prepare chicken, and we're not alone in this, is roasting. Roasting, defined here as cooking uncovered in an oven, most effectively preserves and develops the natural flavors of chicken. And really, when the chore of basting is done away with, as in our recipe for Roasted Chicken with Lemon and Thyme on page 64, it's one of the simplest methods of all.

When roasting a whole chicken, the cooking time may vary depending on the weight of the chicken. Follow the general roasting times (at right) and, near the end of the time limit, give the thigh a poke. If the juices run clear, the chicken is most likely thoroughly cooked. If the juices are slightly pink, slide the chicken back in for additional oven time. It's always wise to take an internal temperature reading to make absolutely certain the chicken is done. The temperature should be between 170 and 180 degrees.

CHICKEN

Name	Weight	Best Use
Broilers	1 to 2½ pounds	Roasting whole
Broilers / Fryers	2½ to 3½ pounds	Roasting, Frying pieces
Roosters / Pullets	3½ to 6½ pounds	Baking, Barbecuing
Hens	8 pounds	Stocks, Chicken Salad, Slow cooking

Weight	Roasting Times
3 pounds	55 to 60 minutes
3½ pounds	60 to 65 minutes
4 to 4½ pounds	65 to 70 minutes

ROASTED CHICKEN WITH LEMON AND THYME

A plain roasted chicken is good; this one is even better. Remember to let your chicken rest a few minutes before carving, as it will continue to cook after it comes from the oven. This rest time allows the juices to redistribute, too, making each slice more moist and tender.

ROASTED CHICKEN WITH LEMON AND THYME	From the Longaberger Pantry
1	tablespoon salt
2	teaspoons fresh ground pepper
2	tablespoons chopped fresh thyme leaves, or
	1 tablespoon dried thyme leaves
	Zest of 1 lemon
1	(3-pound) free-range chicken
2	tablespoons butter, or 1/4 cup olive oil
1	lemon

Mix the salt, pepper, thyme and lemon zest in a small bowl. Rub the chicken with the butter. Season the cavity and the skin with the mixture. Stuff the lemon into the cavity and truss the chicken. Place on a rack in a roasting pan. Roast at 375 degrees for 1 hour or until the juices run clear and the chicken is cooked through. Remove the chicken to a serving platter. Cut the twine and remove with the lemon.

Serves 6

ROASTING WITH RUBS

We love gravy as much as anyone, but more and more people we know are increasingly turning to rubs to add flavor to roasted poultry. Certainly healthier than rich gravies or sauces, rubs are a great way to experiment with ethnic flavors.

What's a rub? There are two kinds. A dry rub is a mixture of salt, crushed or chopped herbs, spices, and aromatics like citrus zest. Sometimes these same ingredients are mixed with oil or yogurt to make a paste. Wet or dry, the mixtures are then rubbed over the uncooked poultry (although they're equally exciting on meat and fish), which is then popped into the refrigerator for several hours or overnight and allowed to absorb the rub's flavors. Rubs can either be left on the food while it cooks or removed before cooking. And remember, your herb-roasted chicken will only be as good as the spices and the herbs that you use. If you're using dried herbs, make sure they're not too old. (Purchase new dry seasonings at least yearly.)

CHICKEN WITH INDIAN SPICE RUB
From the Longaberger Pantry

1	(3-pound) chicken	1 1/2	teaspoons each
1/4	cup olive oil		turmeric and paprika
2	tablespoons	1	teaspoon each
	minced garlic		ground cinnamon,
1	tablespoon ginger		fresh cracked pepper
1	tablespoon		and ground cumin
	kosher salt	1/2	cup plain yogurt

Cut the chicken into pieces, leaving the breast and wing attached and the leg and thigh attached. Combine the olive oil, garlic, ginger, kosher salt, turmeric, paprika, cinnamon, pepper and cumin in a bowl and mix well. Stir in the yogurt. Rub on the chicken pieces. Place in a single layer in a shallow dish. Cover with plastic wrap. Marinate in the refrigerator for 2 to 24 hours. Place on a greased rack in a roasting pan. Roast at 375 degrees for 40 to 50 minutes or until the juices run clear.

CHICKEN WITH SOUTHWESTERN SPICE RUB
From the Longaberger Pantry

1/4	cup pepper	1	tablespoon
1/4	cup paprika		chopped onion
1 1/2	tablespoons salt	1	tablespoon cumin seeds
1	tablespoon chopped	1	(3-pound) chicken
	garlic		Stuffing

Mix the pepper, paprika, salt, garlic, onion and cumin seeds in a bowl. Rub on the chicken. Chill, covered, for 2 to 24 hours. Fill the chicken cavity with stuffing. Truss the chicken and roast following the directions on the previous page until a meat thermometer inserted into the thickest portion registers 170 to 180 degrees.

CHICKEN WITH MEDITERRANEAN SPICE RUB
From the Longaberger Pantry

2	tablespoons olive oil
1/2	cup kalamata olives, pitted, chopped, mashed
1	tablespoon each chopped orange zest and garlic
1	tablespoon each fennel seeds and oregano leaves
1	(3-pound) chicken, butterflied

Mix the olive oil, olives, orange zest, garlic, fennel seeds and oregano in a bowl. Rub on the chicken. Chill, covered, for 2 to 24 hours. Roast at 375 degrees for 40 to 50 minutes or until the juices run clear.

Chicken Vegetable Potpie

Is there anything that says "home" more than tender chicken and garden vegetables gathered into a silky sauce and tucked neatly beneath a blanket of a golden, flaky crust? We think not. Our version of the classic potpie can be largely prepared a day ahead of time. The final step—preparing the phyllo dough crust—should be done just before the pie gets popped into the oven.

CHICKEN VEGETABLE POTPIE
From the Longaberger Pantry

2	cups chopped onions	4	cups bite-size roasted chicken pieces
1/2	cup (1 stick) unsalted butter	3	carrots, diced, blanched, drained (2 cups)
1/2	cup flour		
1	cup half-and-half		
2	cups chicken stock	2	ribs celery, chopped (1 1/3 cups)
1/4	cup chopped fresh parsley	6	small red potatoes, boiled, drained, cut into bite-size pieces
1	teaspoon dried thyme		
2	teaspoons sea salt	1	small bunch broccoli, chopped, blanched, drained (2 cups)
1/2	teaspoon ground pepper		
8	ounces button mushrooms, quartered	1	(10-ounce) package frozen peas, thawed
		3	phyllo sheets
1	tablespoon unsalted butter	6	tablespoons unsalted butter, melted

Sauté the onions in 1/2 cup butter in a skillet until translucent. Add the flour. Cook for 1 minute, stirring constantly. Add the half-and-half, chicken stock, parsley, thyme, sea salt and pepper. Cook until thickened, stirring constantly. Remove from the heat.

Sauté the mushrooms in 1 tablespoon butter in a skillet until tender. Add the chicken, sautéed mushrooms, carrots, celery, potatoes, broccoli and peas to the sauce. Butter our 9×13-inch Baking Dish. Pour in the chicken mixture. Layer the phyllo sheets over the top, brushing some of the 6 tablespoons melted butter between each layer and over the top. Pinch the phyllo sheets to the rim of the dish to seal. Brush the top layer again with the remaining melted butter. Bake at 350 degrees for 45 to 50 minutes or until golden brown.

Serves 8 to 10

PREPARATION TIP

WHAT? NO ROASTED CHICKEN ON HAND?

Relax, you can still have Chicken Vegetable Potpie tonight. Just swing by the grocery store and pick up roasted chickens or turkey breasts from the deli.

POPEYE'S HONEY PECAN CHICKEN SALAD

This recipe alone is worth the price of the book. It's a popular lunch choice at a diner in our hometown of Dresden, Ohio, called Popeye's. (Popeye was the childhood nickname of Longaberger® Founder Dave Longaberger.) Next time you roast a chicken, prepare an extra one to use later in the week for this soon-to-be family favorite.

POPEYE'S HONEY PECAN CHICKEN SALAD

From the Longaberger Pantry

1	cup mayonnaise
1/2	cup relish
2	tablespoons minced onion
1	tablespoon honey
1 1/2	tablespoons sugar
1	teaspoon salt
1/4	teaspoon white pepper
3/4	cup chopped celery
3/4	cup toasted pecans, coarsely chopped
1 1/2	pounds chopped cooked chicken (about 4 cups)

Combine the mayonnaise, relish, onion, honey, sugar, salt and white pepper in a bowl and mix well. Stir in the celery and pecans. Fold in the chicken. Adjust the seasonings to taste. Chill, covered, in the refrigerator. Serve on crusty French bread rolls with potato chips and carrot sticks, or on a bed of salad greens, garnished with a bunch of red grapes.

Serves 6 to 8

What's for Supper?

Ever in a quandary about what to fix for "supper," as many families in our neck of the woods call their evening meal? Consider borrowing a page from Grandma Bonnie's meal-planning book. She let each of her twelve children choose the menu for one meal a month. She says her son, Dave, often requested pancakes. "And you could always count on him being at the table for that meal!" she remembers. Years later, Dave still enjoyed playing a part in menus. From his first restaurant, Popeye's, right up to the many restaurants at the Longaberger Homestead®, Dave would inquire of customers: "How do you like that new menu item?" Then he'd say, pointing to one of the waitresses, "It was all her doing!"

Why not get your family involved in menu planning? While you may encounter some interesting combinations (bologna and oatmeal, anyone?), everyone soon learns that it's not as easy as it seems to combine different tastes, colors, and textures of foods to create an appetizing plate. And don't stop the family involvement in the planning stage. Invite the little menu-makers into the kitchen to help cook the dinners they dream up.

CHICKEN PICCATA

Here's a fresh version of an Italian classic that never grows old. A quick way to dress up plain old chicken, the sunny color and zingy flavors of lemon and capers in this dish marry well with pilafs, potatoes, or pastas. When you're in the mood, substitute the chicken for fresh fish fillets, veal cutlets, or turkey medallions.

EVER TRIED FRIED CAPERS?

We think they lend a delicious crunch to garden salads or cooked vegetables. They're easy to prepare, too. Just dry a jarful of capers in paper towels and toss them in a pan of hot peanut oil for a few seconds. Fish the capers out of the oil with a slotted spoon and drain them on paper towels. But don't salt them—they're salty enough!

CHICKEN PICCATA	From the Longaberger Pantry
1 1/2 cups flour	
1 teaspoon salt	
1/4 teaspoon pepper	
8 (4-ounce) boneless skinless chicken breasts	
2 tablespoons butter	
1 tablespoon vegetable oil	
1/3 cup water	
3 tablespoons lemon juice	
1 lemon, thinly sliced	
3 tablespoons drained capers	
3 tablespoons chopped fresh parsley	

Combine the flour, salt and pepper in a shallow dish. Pound the chicken 1/4 inch thick. Dredge the chicken in the flour mixture, shaking off the excess. Heat the butter and oil in a large skillet over medium heat. Add the chicken. Cook for 3 minutes per side or until the juices run clear. Remove the chicken to a plate and cover to keep warm. Add the water to the skillet. Cook for 1 minute, stirring to deglaze the skillet. Add the lemon juice. Bring to a boil, stirring constantly. Return the chicken to the skillet. Place the lemon slices over the chicken. Cook for 5 minutes or until the sauce thickens. Top with the capers. Sprinkle with the parsley.
Serves 8

VARIATION

For *Lemon Ginger Chicken,* combine 1/2 cup fresh lemon juice, 6 garlic cloves, minced, and 2 tablespoons grated fresh gingerroot in a bowl. Add the pounded chicken. Marinate, covered, in the refrigerator for 2 to 6 hours. Drain the chicken, reserving the marinade for the sauce. Pat the chicken dry.

Follow the directions above for dredging and cooking the chicken. Add 1/4 cup chicken stock to the skillet instead of the water. Cook for 1 minute, stirring to deglaze the skillet. Stir in the reserved marinade. Bring to a boil. Return the chicken to the skillet. Sprinkle with 1 teaspoon paprika, 1/2 teaspoon ginger, 1/4 teaspoon pepper and 2 tablespoons brown sugar. Cook until the sauce thickens. Adjust the seasonings to taste if necessary.

HERB-CRUSTED TURKEY BREAST

Turkey is another superb source of low-fat protein, for all the same reasons that chicken is. We prefer preparing a turkey breast over a whole bird because it requires less cooking time, which in turn results in a moister meat. Any leftovers can reappear tomorrow in turkey sandwiches or in our home-style Creamy Turkey Hash (facing page).

HERB-CRUSTED TURKEY BREAST

From the Longaberger Pantry

3	tablespoons chopped fresh rosemary, or	1	tablespoon ground pepper
1½	tablespoons dried rosemary	2	teaspoons salt
3	tablespoons chopped fresh thyme, or	1	(6- to 7-pound) turkey breast
1½	tablespoons dried thyme	2	tablespoons vegetable oil
3	tablespoons chopped fresh parsley, or	6	tablespoons butter, melted
1½	tablespoons dried parsley	2	cups canned reduced-sodium chicken broth

Mix the rosemary, thyme, parsley, pepper and salt in a small bowl. Pat the turkey dry with paper towels and place on a rack in a large roasting pan. Brush the turkey with the oil. Rub the herb mixture over the turkey.

Position the oven rack in the lowest one-third of the oven and preheat to 450 degrees. Drizzle the melted butter over the turkey. Pour 1 cup of the broth into the pan. Roast the turkey for 20 minutes. Remove the turkey from the oven and cover with foil. Reduce the oven temperature to 350 degrees. Return the turkey to the oven. Roast for 1 hour longer. Remove the foil from the turkey. Pour the remaining 1 cup broth into the pan. Continue roasting the turkey for 40 to 45 minutes or until a meat thermometer inserted into the thickest portion registers 180 degrees, basting occasionally with the pan juices. Remove the turkey to a platter and tent with foil. Let stand for 30 minutes. Reserve the liquid in the pan for gravy if desired.

Serves 8 to 10

CREAMY TURKEY HASH

From the
Longaberger
Pantry

4	cups chopped cooked turkey	1/2	cup grated Parmesan cheese
4	cups cooked rice (use a mixture of brown, white and/or wild rice)	1/4	cup chopped fresh Italian parsley
		1	cup heavy cream
1	pound button mushrooms, sliced, sautéed	2	eggs
		1	teaspoon paprika
1/2	cup chopped onion, sautéed		Salt and pepper to taste

Combine the turkey, rice, mushrooms, onion, Parmesan cheese and parsley in a bowl and toss to mix well. Whisk the cream, eggs, paprika, salt and pepper in a bowl. Pour over the turkey mixture. Let stand for 15 to 20 minutes. Spoon into a baking dish. Bake at 350 degrees for 20 to 25 minutes or until bubbly. Broil for 3 to 5 minutes or until the top is golden brown.

Serves 4 to 6

HEALTHY TURKEY LASAGNA

Good cooks love lasagna because it can be assembled ahead of time, then baked without much fuss right before a family gathering or casual dinner party. We make it in our 9×13-inch Baking Dish, which is made of vitrified china to go safely from refrigerator to oven to table. The hot dish slips right into our handsome 9×13-inch Serving Solutions™ Basket.

VARIATIONS

You don't need lasagna noodles to make lasagna—use penne, ziti, or bow tie pasta. Either mix or layer the ingredients, then bake as directed.

Also try replacing the ground turkey with the same amount of ground beef, sausage, ground pork, or cooked shrimp and scallops. If you use seafood, shorten the baking time by 5 to 10 minutes. The lasagna may be assembled up to 1 day in advance and refrigerated. Bake chilled seafood lasagna for 30 to 35 minutes. If it's made with beef, pork or poultry, bake chilled lasagna for 40 to 45 minutes.

HEALTHY TURKEY LASAGNA

From the Longaberger Pantry

1	(26-ounce) jar no-fat garlic and herb pasta sauce
1	(14-ounce) can diced tomatoes
1	(8-ounce) can mushroom stems and pieces, drained
2	(10-ounce) packages frozen chopped spinach, thawed
1	pound tenderloin of turkey breast, thinly sliced
1	tablespoon olive oil
1/2	cup chopped celery
1/2	cup chopped green onions
1/2	cup chopped green and red bell peppers
16	ounces reduced-fat cottage cheese
16	ounces reduced-fat ricotta cheese
1/4	cup grated Parmesan cheese
9	cooked lasagna noodles
1	cup no-fat mozzarella cheese
	Tomato slices, fresh parsley and ground pepper

Combine the pasta sauce, tomatoes and mushrooms in a bowl and mix well.

Squeeze the spinach to remove excess liquid. Sauté the turkey in the olive oil in a skillet for 4 to 5 minutes. Add the celery, green onions, bell peppers and spinach. Cook until the vegetables are tender-crisp.

Combine the cottage cheese, ricotta cheese and Parmesan cheese in a bowl and mix well.

To assemble, spread 1/2 cup of the sauce mixture in our 9×13-inch Baking Dish sprayed with nonstick cooking spray. Layer 3 of the lasagna noodles, 1/3 of the cheese mixture, 1/2 of the turkey mixture and 1/3 of the remaining pasta sauce mixture in the prepared dish. Continue layering with 3 lasagna noodles, 1/2 of the remaining cheese mixture, remaining turkey mixture and 1/2 of the remaining pasta sauce. Top the layers with the remaining lasagna noodles, remaining cheese mixture and remaining pasta sauce mixture. Bake, covered, at 350 degrees for 20 minutes. Uncover and bake for 10 minutes longer. Sprinkle with the mozzarella cheese. Garnish with tomato slices, parsley and pepper.

Serves 8 to 10

GRILLED SALMON WITH ROASTED RED PEPPER SAUCE

Grilled salmon is a healthy yet hearty alternative to meat. We suggest preparing this pretty salmon dish on the very day that you purchase the salmon. It's a good idea to "ice" the fish until you're ready to cook it: Rinse the fish well with water, pop it into a plastic food storage bag, and either lay it on ice or immerse it in a panful of ice in the refrigerator.

HEALTHY TIP
ROBUST RED PEPPER SAUCE

For a sauce that's big on texture and light on fat, follow the recipe for Roasted Red Pepper Sauce (at right), eliminating the cream. Fold in 2 tablespoons drained capers, 1/3 cup slivered imported olives, 1/4 cup snipped fresh basil leaves and a grinding or two of fresh cracked pepper to taste.

GRILLED SALMON	From the Longaberger Pantry
4 salmon fillets	
1 tablespoon vegetable oil	
Salt and pepper to taste	
Roasted Red Pepper Sauce (below)	

Rub the salmon with the oil. Sprinkle with salt and pepper. Place on a hot grill rack. Grill for 3 to 5 minutes per side or until the salmon flakes easily, turning once. Spoon Roasted Red Pepper Sauce on each serving plate. Top with the grilled salmon.

Serves 4

ROASTED RED PEPPER SAUCE	From the Longaberger Pantry
2 large red bell peppers	
1 tablespoon vegetable oil	
1 garlic clove	
2 tablespoons olive oil	
1/4 cup heavy cream	

Cut the bell peppers into halves lengthwise and discard the core and seeds. Brush the outside of the bell pepper halves with the vegetable oil. Place on a rack in a broiler pan. Broil for 10 to 15 minutes or until the bell pepper skins are blistered and blackened all over. Place in a nonrecycled paper bag or sealable plastic bag and seal. Let stand for 15 minutes or until cool. Remove from the bag and remove the skins. Combine the roasted bell peppers, garlic and olive oil in a blender container. Process until puréed. Add the cream and process until blended.

Makes 1 1/2 cups

PISTACHIO-ENCRUSTED WALLEYE

Dredge almost any food in a coating of flour, crumbs, nuts or grated cheese and it will stay more moist and tender when you cook it. This crunchy coating created by the chef at the Longaberger Golf Club®, makes a lovely brown crust that contrasts nicely with the light, flaky fish inside.

SERVING TIP

WHAT GOES WITH WALLEYE?

Try Wasabi Mashed Potatoes (facing page). Ever heard of wasabi? It's a root from Japan that is mixed with soy sauce as a condiment with sushi. But, surprise—wasabi also makes mashed potatoes more interesting. Fresh wasabi is rarely available, and you may even have difficulty finding wasabi powder. If so, try horseradish instead. Same kick, slightly different flavor.

PISTACHIO-ENCRUSTED WALLEYE		From the Longaberger Pantry	
1	cup flour	2	eggs, beaten
1	teaspoon salt	2	cups shelled white
1	teaspoon pepper		pistachios, finely
2	tablespoons		chopped
	lemon juice	1/4	cup vegetable oil
1	tablespoon		Leek Sauce (below)
	Worcestershire sauce		Chopped fresh
4	(6-ounce) skinned		parsley (optional)
	walleye fillets		

Mix the flour, salt and pepper in a sealable plastic bag. Combine the lemon juice and Worcestershire sauce in a bowl and mix well. Pour over the fish in a shallow dish. Marinate for 10 minutes. Drain the fish and pat dry. Dredge 2 fillets at a time in the flour mixture and then dip in the eggs; dip in the pistachios. Repeat the process. Place the fillets on a baking sheet. Chill, covered, for 10 to 30 minutes.

Heat the vegetable oil in a cast-iron skillet. Fry the fillets in batches in the hot oil for 3 minutes on each side or until the fillets flake easily, draining and wiping the skillet clean with paper towels between batches. Place the fillets on a warm platter. Drizzle with Leek Sauce. Garnish with chopped fresh parsley.

Serves 4

LEEK SAUCE		From the Longaberger Pantry	
1/4	cup (1/2 stick)	1	cup whiskey
	unsalted butter	1/4	cup (1/2 stick)
1	cup chopped leeks		unsalted butter
1	cup chicken or fish		Salt to taste
	stock		

Melt 1/4 cup butter in a cast-iron skillet. Add the leeks. Sauté until translucent. Add the stock and whiskey. Cook until the sauce is reduced to 1/2 cup. Remove from the heat. Whisk in 1/4 cup butter. Add salt to taste if needed.

Makes 3/4 cup

WASABI MASHED POTATOES

From the
Longaberger
Pantry

2¹/2   pounds potatoes, peeled

¹/2   cup (1 stick) unsalted butter

1   cup heavy cream

3   to 5 ounces wasabi powder,
     or ¹/4 cup horseradish,
     or to taste

Cook the potatoes in boiling water to cover in a saucepan until tender. Bring the butter and cream to a simmer in a saucepan. Drain the potatoes and place in a mixing bowl. Beat at low speed until mashed. Add the cream mixture gradually, beating constantly until smooth and creamy. Stir in the wasabi powder, adjusting the amount to suit your taste.

Serves 4

LEMON GARLIC SHRIMP STIR-FRY

Close your eyes and imagine a riot of primary-colored vegetables nestled on a stark white bed of orzo, rice, or noodles. Now imagine the first bite of those crisp-cooked vegetables rollicking around your mouth in a snappy, lemony sauce. You've just imagined this recipe. Preparation is less than 45 minutes and the vegetables can be varied according to what's freshest at hand at any given moment.

LEMON GARLIC SHRIMP STIR-FRY	From the Longaberger Pantry
2	tablespoons olive oil
1	red or yellow bell pepper, cut into julienne strips
1	medium zucchini, cut into 1/2-inch half-moon slices
1	pound uncooked peeled shrimp
4	garlic cloves, minced
1/2	cup diagonally sliced scallions
6	ounces snow peas
1/4	cup lemon juice
	Zest of 1 lemon
	Salt and pepper to taste
1/2	cup fresh parsley, coarsely chopped
1/4	cup chopped chives

Heat the olive oil in a wok or large skillet. Add the bell pepper and zucchini. Stir-fry for 3 minutes. Add the shrimp, garlic and scallions. Stir-fry over high heat for a few more minutes. Add the snow peas. Stir-fry until the shrimp begin to curl. Add the lemon juice and zest. Stir-fry until the shrimp turn pink. Remove to a serving platter using a slotted spoon. Season with salt and pepper. Sprinkle with parsley and chives. Serve with orzo, rice or noodles.

Serves 4 to 6

GARLIC AND ROSEMARY ROASTED PORK TENDERLOIN

It's true what they say about pork: It really is a lean alternative. It's at its best when infused with bold flavors, as in this herb-encrusted roast. Marinate the tenderloin today, roast and serve it tomorrow, then serve it again for lunch the next day—cold, thinly sliced, with good bread and a pot of mustard. Leftovers? What leftovers?

WHAT IS MOJO?

Mojo (pronounced "mo-ho") is the Spanish word for a marinade made with vinegar or citrus juices, garlic, and selected seasonings. Although there are a multitude of mojon recipes, we chose this kicky, citrusy one to get you started. Stored in the fridge, it can be made up to three days ahead of time.

ROASTED PORK TENDERLOIN			From the Longaberger Pantry
1/4	cup olive oil	2	tablespoons chopped fresh thyme
2	tablespoons balsamic vinegar	2	tablespoons chopped fresh parsley
1	tablespoon cider vinegar		
3	large garlic cloves, chopped	2	tablespoons Dijon mustard
1/4	cup chopped fresh rosemary	1	(14- to 16-ounce) pork tenderloin

Process the olive oil, balsamic vinegar, cider vinegar, garlic, rosemary, thyme, parsley and Dijon mustard in a food processor until the herbs are finely chopped. Place the pork in a heavy sealable plastic bag. Pour the marinade over the pork and seal the bag. Marinate in the refrigerator for 8 to 12 hours, turning occasionally. Drain the pork, discarding the marinade. Place the pork on a rack in a small roasting pan. Roast at 375 degrees for 25 minutes or until a meat thermometer inserted in the center registers 160 degrees. Let stand for 5 minutes. Cut the pork into thin slices to serve.

Serves 4

V A R I A T I O N

MOJO			From the Longaberger Pantry
12	small garlic cloves, finely chopped	1 1/2	teaspoons ground toasted cumin seeds
1	teaspoon sea salt	1	teaspoon pepper
1/4	cup fresh orange juice	1/2	cup extra-virgin olive oil
1/4	cup fresh lime juice		

Purée the garlic and sea salt in a blender. Add the orange juice, lime juice, cumin and pepper and blend well. Add the olive oil in a fine stream, processing constantly until emulsified. Use to marinate a pork loin in the refrigerator for 1 to 3 hours. Continue following the directions above.

Makes 1 cup

PREPARATION
TIP
MARINATE IT!

Marinades are a good trick to keep up your sleeve because of the amazing effects they have on meat. They tenderize, add exceptional flavors, and the extra moisture from marinades helps keep meats from drying out during cooking. Usually a marinade is discarded after the uncooked meat has been removed from it. If you want to serve the marinade as a sauce, be sure to boil it for several minutes first.

Here's another recipe that's often requested at the Longaberger Golf Club®. These satisfying chops have a fresh-apple sauce that's perfect with the golf club restaurant's Sweet Potato Fries (below) and a side of fresh, steamed green beans. One taste and you'll no longer think that baseball-park soft pretzels only go with mustard.

SERVING TIP

SWEET POTATO FRIES

For *Sweet Potato Fries,* peel 4 large sweet potatoes and cut into sticks. Fry in small batches in hot vegetable oil in a skillet until tender; drain on paper towels. Mix 1/2 cup packed brown sugar, 1/2 cup cinnamon, 1 teaspoon kosher salt and 1/4 teaspoon pepper in a bowl. Add the hot sweet potatoes and toss to coat. During the holiday season, add a pinch or two of nutmeg or allspice to the mix of dry seasonings. Very festive!

PRETZEL-STUFFED PORK CHOPS	From the Longaberger Pantry
4	(10-ounce) pork loin chops, butterflied
	Salt and pepper to taste
4	large soft pretzels, cut into 1/2-inch pieces
2	large red apples, finely chopped
1	large red onion, finely chopped
1/2	cup chopped fresh rosemary
1/4	cup chopped fresh basil
1	cup apple juice
1/2	cup cola
2	cups each apple juice and cola
6	garlic cloves, peeled
2	red apples, cut into 2-inch pieces
1/4	cup packed brown sugar
1	teaspoon cinnamon

Season the pork with salt and pepper. Combine the pretzels, chopped apples, onion, rosemary, basil, 1 cup apple juice and 1/2 cup cola in a bowl and mix well. Divide into 4 equal portions. Stuff 1 portion into each pork chop, letting the stuffing overflow for effect. Pour 2 cups apple juice and 2 cups cola into a baking dish. Add the garlic, apple pieces, brown sugar and cinnamon. Add the stuffed pork chops. Bake, covered, at 350 degrees for 25 minutes or until a meat thermometer registers 160 degrees, checking for doneness at 10- to 15-minute intervals. Remove the pork chops to a heated platter. Purée the pan drippings with a hand tool or in a blender. Pour into a saucepan. Cook until reduced and thickened. Ladle over the pork chops.

Serves 4

VARIATION

For *Pineapple Sauce,* add 1/2 cup drained pineapple tidbits and 1 cup spiced dark rum to the pan drippings above. Pour into a saucepan. Cook over high heat until reduced and thickened. Serve over the pork chops.

How About a Round of World-Class Golf?

When J. W. Longaberger, Dave's dad, decided to retire, the last thing he wanted to do was sit around on the porch, watching the world go by. Instead, he applied for a job as a guard at the local swimming pool, a popular gathering place for gossip and horseplay, and maybe a hot dog and a soda or two. In that same community-minded spirit, The Longaberger® Company has invested millions of dollars over the years in local recreational facilities, roads and sidewalks, the Bonnie Longaberger Senior Center, and local school development.

In 1998, Dave decided that what the neighborhood really needed was not just one, but two world-class golf courses. It's hard to say whether the idea sprang from his desire to create more ways for people to gather and play, eat and joke, or to simply further

indulge his passion for throwing dinner rolls. But whatever his reasons, the result of Dave's dream is now one of *Golf Magazine's* top-10-rated public courses in the country. Every year, thousands of players find their way to the greens and fairways of the Longaberger Golf Club® near Newark, Ohio. Designed by renowned architect Arthur Hills, this remarkable course includes five sets of tees, bent grass tees, greens and fairways, a 25-acre practice facility, a short game area, and two practice greens. And there's this unique benefit: Our course is environmentally managed and is in qualification for certification in the Audubon International Signature Cooperative Sanctuary Program. Dave thought we should strive for the best and ... oh, yeah, leave the flora and fauna as untouched as possible.

CHINESE BRAISED BEEF SHORT RIBS WITH GINGER SOY GLAZE

Short ribs are usually a good buy because they boast a good amount of flavorful meat, which only improves with browning and roasting. Serve these lip-smackin' ribs with roasted mashed sweet potatoes and braised red cabbage. On another night, serve them with spicy sesame noodles and garlic green beans, and no one will know they've eaten the same thing twice.

CHINESE BRAISED BEEF SHORT RIBS	From the Longaberger Pantry
5	pounds beef short ribs
	Salt to taste
3	tablespoons Chinese five-spice powder
	Vegetable oil for browning
4	garlic cloves, chopped
4	small onions, unpeeled, chopped
6	small carrots, chopped
	Pepper to taste
2	cups chicken stock
1	cup orange juice
1/4	cup rice wine vinegar
	Ginger Soy Glaze (facing page)

Cut the beef into 1-inch rib pieces. Season with salt and Chinese five-spice powder. Heat the oil in a 6-quart heavy ovenproof kettle over medium-high heat; do not allow to smoke. Brown the beef in batches in an uncrowded single layer in the kettle. Remove to a heated platter. Drain the pan drippings, reserving 2 tablespoons in the kettle. Add the garlic, onions, carrots, salt and pepper. Sauté over medium heat until light brown. Add the chicken stock, orange juice and vinegar. Bring to a boil, stirring constantly. Return the beef to the kettle, squeezing tightly into a single layer. Braise, covered, at 350 degrees for 2 hours or until tender. Remove the ribs to a platter using a tong and keep warm. Brush with Ginger Soy Glaze. Pour the cooking liquid through a fine sieve set over a saucepan. Discard the solids and skim. Boil if needed for the desired consistency until slightly thickened. Serve over the beef.

Serves 4 to 6

V A R I A T I O N

For *Braised Beef Short Ribs* (pictured), prepare the ribs as above except dredge the beef pieces in a mixture of flour, salt and pepper instead of the Chinese five-spice powder; brown in 1/4 cup bacon drippings instead of the vegetable oil; substitute 3 cups beef broth for the chicken stock, 1 cup orange juice and rice wine vinegar; substitute 1/2 teaspoon crumbled dried rosemary for the salt and pepper; and omit brushing with the Ginger Soy Glaze.

GINGER SOY GLAZE

From the
Longaberger
Pantry

1	cup orange juice	2	tablespoons rice vinegar
1/2	cup water		
1/4	cup maple syrup	2	tablespoons soy sauce
1/4	cup honey		
1/4	cup packed brown sugar	1	tablespoon grated fresh gingerroot
1	cinnamon stick		

Combine the orange juice, water, syrup, honey, brown sugar, cinnamon stick, vinegar, soy sauce and gingerroot in a heavy saucepan. Bring to a boil. Cook until the mixture is reduced by 1/2. Remove from the heat. Discard the cinnamon stick. Let stand until cool. The glaze may be prepared several days in advance and stored in the refrigerator.

Serves 6

PAN-SEARED STEAKS WITH MUSTARD SAUCE

We know that beef tenderloin is expensive. But it's so lean, with so little waste, we still think it's a good buy, especially when there's company coming. Traditionally served with roasted potatoes and asparagus, these steaks retain their best flavor—as all steaks do—when served rare to medium-rare.

SERVING TIP

TRY MUSHROOM SAUCE INSTEAD

When you make Pan-Seared Steaks again (and you will), serve the steaks with Mushroom Sauce (at right) instead of the Mustard Sauce (above right).

STEAKS WITH MUSTARD SAUCE	From the Longaberger Pantry
1/2 cup heavy cream	
4 teaspoons dry mustard	
2 teaspoons sugar	
2 tablespoons white wine	
1 cup sour cream	
Coarse salt	
4 (6-ounce) beef tenderloin steaks, cut 1 inch thick	

Combine the cream, dry mustard, sugar and wine in a bowl and mix well. Stir in the sour cream. Chill, covered, in the refrigerator until ready to serve.

Turn on the exhaust fan to capture the smoke this searing process will produce. Heat a large cast-iron or heavy skillet over medium-high heat until nearly smoking. Sprinkle coarse salt in the skillet and add the steaks. Sear for 3 minutes on each side for medium-rare. Remove from the skillet. Serve with the mustard sauce.

Serves 4

V A R I A T I O N

MUSHROOM SAUCE FOR STEAKS			From the Longaberger Pantry
2	tablespoons minced shallots	2	tablespoons red wine vinegar
1	tablespoon olive oil	1	cup beef stock
4	ounces shiitake mushrooms, quartered	2	teaspoons tomato paste
8	ounces button mushrooms, quartered	1	teaspoon salt
1/4	cup cabernet sauvignon	1	teaspoon freshly cracked pepper

Brown the shallots in the olive oil in a heavy sauté pan. Add the mushrooms. Sauté until brown. Add the wine, vinegar, beef stock and tomato paste. Simmer for 5 minutes. Add salt and pepper.

Serves 4

GRILLED FLANK STEAK

Ready to fire up the grill? Think beyond basic burgers and chicken to flank steak. Flank steak is a flavorful, lean, and inexpensive cut of beef, which takes on a wonderful smoky-seared flavor when grilled. Flank steak is usually marinated, as it is in this recipe, to make it more tender. Try not to overcook the steak (it should still be pink inside), and when slicing, cut diagonally against the grain.

GRILLED FLANK STEAK	From the Longaberger Pantry
1	onion, sliced
3/4	cup white wine
1/4	cup white wine vinegar
2	tablespoons olive or vegetable oil
1	tablespoon chopped fresh basil
1/2	teaspoon salt
	Crushed hot red pepper flakes to taste
1	to 1 1/2 pounds flank steak, trimmed
1	garlic clove, chopped

Combine the onion, wine, vinegar, olive oil, basil, salt and red pepper flakes in a shallow glass baking dish and mix well. Rub both sides of the steak evenly with garlic. Place in the dish, turning to coat. Marinate, covered, in the refrigerator for 2 to 24 hours. Drain the steak, discarding the marinade. Pat dry with paper towels. Place on a grill rack. Grill 4 inches from the heat source for about 6 minutes per side for medium. Let stand for 10 minutes. Cut into thin slices across the grain before serving.

Serves 6

VARIATIONS

For *Asian Flank Steak,* substitute chopped green onions for the onion and 1/2 cup soy sauce for the wine. Use 1/2 cup orange juice instead of the white wine vinegar; substitute sesame oil for the olive oil. Add 1 tablespoon grated fresh gingerroot. Add the remaining ingredients and continue as above.

For *Horseradish Caper Flank Steak,* mix together 5 tablespoons sour cream, 1 tablespoon prepared horseradish, 1 minced garlic clove, 1 teaspoon drained and chopped capers and fresh cracked pepper to taste in a bowl. Add the steak and marinate, covered, in the refrigerator for 1 to 2 days. Cook as directed above.

For *Cold Flank Steak Salad* (pictured), cut 1 pound chilled cooked flank steak into thin slices. To the flank steak add 2 fresh, ripe tomatoes, peeled, chopped, and 1 medium zucchini, chopped. Add 1/2 cup Basic Vinaigrette (page 28), 2 tablespoons Dijon mustard, 2 teaspoons chopped fresh tarragon and 1/2 cup chopped fresh Italian parsley leaves and toss to coat. Serve on a bed of salad greens.

THE GREAT AMERICAN HAMBURGER

Ground beef in a bun may not be glamorous, but it can be great family fun. Originating in Hamburg, Germany, burgers are now probably more American than hot dogs or apple pie. Everyone loves them with the ubiquitous fries, but don't dismiss the idea of crispy fried onions and a mixed vegetable slaw on the side, either. With apologies to nutritionists, we think the juiciest burgers are made with beef that's not too lean. Go easy on the seasonings, too, as herbs, onions, bread crumbs, and the like hide the natural flavor of ground beef. Pile the zesty stuff on top of your burgers instead, like we do with our Caesar Burgers (at right). Or try them stuffed like our Atomic Burgers (also at right).

THE GREAT AMERICAN HAMBURGER	From the Longaberger Pantry
2 pounds ground chuck	
1 shallot, minced	
2 teaspoons salt	
1 teaspoon ground pepper	
Salt and pepper to taste	

Combine the ground chuck, shallot, 2 teaspoons salt and 1 teaspoon pepper in a bowl and mix gently. Shape into four 8-ounce patties 1 1/4 inches thick. (For optimal tenderness, try not to handle the ground chuck too much.) Place in a single layer on a platter. Chill, covered, in the refrigerator. Uncover and season with salt and pepper to taste. Make a small indentation in the center of each burger to help retain its shape. Place the patties on a grill rack. Grill over medium-hot coals until a meat thermometer inserted into the center of each patty registers 160 degrees, turning once. (Do not press the burgers as they cook or the juices will escape.)

Makes 4 hamburgers

VARIATIONS

For *Caesar Burgers* (pictured), prepare 1/2 of the dressing in Caesar Salad (page 32) and toss with 1/2 of the shredded romaine. To assemble, place each patty on the bottom of a toasted hamburger bun. Layer 1 or 2 tomato slices, a mound of Caesar Salad and shredded Parmesan cheese on each patty. If you are feeling brave, throw in a few anchovies. Replace the top of the toasted hamburger bun.

For *Atomic Burgers,* shape the ground chuck into 8 patties 1/2 inch thick. Make a small indentation in the center of each beef patty. Combine 6 ounces of crumbled bleu cheese, 2 tablespoons butter, 2 tablespoons chopped fresh parsley, 2 teaspoons chopped fresh garlic and 1/2 teaspoon thyme in a bowl and mix well. Divide into 4 equal portions. Place 1 portion in the center of each of 4 beef patties. Top with the remaining beef patties, pressing the edges together to seal. Season with salt and pepper. Chill, covered, until ready to grill.

LONGABERGER HOMESTEAD®
MEAT LOAF

Longaberger Homestead Restaurant serves family-style meals like your grandmother used to make. Like this meat loaf, for instance. Sometimes we like it served with garlic mashed potatoes; sometimes we like it with baked potatoes and roasted carrots and onions. Oh, and we doubled the recipe for you so you'll have an extra loaf to wrap and freeze. Or slice it the next day for cold meat loaf sandwiches smothered in ketchup. Pass extra napkins.

SMART TIP

MORE ABOUT MEAT LOAF

Meat loaf is best prepared with a combination of 50 percent beef, 25 percent veal and 25 percent pork. If ground veal isn't available, use 75 percent beef and 25 percent pork. The larger proportion of beef is key to a meat loaf that's firm and slices easily. For a perfectly moist, delectably crumbly meat loaf, choose 80 percent lean beef—not 100 percent lean beef—and use a gentle hand when mixing the ingredients together.

	LONGABERGER HOMESTEAD® MEAT LOAF	From the Longaberger Pantry
3	pounds ground beef	
1/2	cup chopped onion	
2	tablespoons chopped celery	
1/2	teaspoon horseradish	
1/2	cup tomato sauce	
1/2	cup ketchup	
1	tablespoon dry mustard	
1/2	tablespoon garlic	
1/2	tablespoon Worcestershire sauce	
1/2	tablespoon salt	
1	teaspoon pepper	
3	eggs	
3/4	cup bread crumbs	

Crumble the ground beef into a large bowl. Add the onion, celery, horseradish, tomato sauce, ketchup, dry mustard, garlic, Worcestershire sauce, salt and pepper and mix thoroughly. Add the eggs and bread crumbs and mix well. Divide into 2 equal portions. Shape each portion into a loaf. Place in 2 of our Loaf Dishes. Bake at 350 degrees for 1 hour or until a meat thermometer inserted in the center of each loaf registers 160 degrees. Cool for 8 to 10 minutes before serving.

Serves 16

VARIATIONS

For *Hickory Smoked Meat Loaf,* wrap the meat loaf in bacon before baking for a wonderful smoky flavor.

For *Spicy Meat Loaves,* decrease the ground beef to 2 1/2 pounds and add 8 ounces Italian sausage.

For *Turkey Meat Loaves,* substitute fresh ground turkey for the beef. Add 1/2 cup chopped celery, 1/2 cup chopped bell peppers and 1 teaspoon cumin. Bake until a meat thermometer inserted in the center of each loaf registers 165 degrees.

For *Hot Texas Meat Loaves,* substitute your favorite salsa for the ketchup and add 1 teaspoon cumin and 1/2 cup chopped green onions. Reserve 2 tablespoons of the salsa for brushing the top of the hot meat loaves.

From Chestnut Street to Longaberger Homestead®

From the earliest days of The Longaberger® Company, people have come from miles around just to see our talented basketmakers create our one-of-a-kind collectibles. At first Dave Longaberger himself conducted tours of our first facility on Chestnut Street in pretty little Dresden, Ohio, but it wasn't long before his daughter Rachel took over. By 1991, almost before we knew it, more than 12,000 tourists were coming to visit each year! To help welcome them, Popeye's Restaurant, a lively diner-like lunch place that borrowed Dave's childhood nickname, was there to serve a hearty meal. Today, hundreds of thousands of visitors tour our massive Manufacturing Campus each year, then head just down the road to the Longaberger Homestead.

Newly opened in 2000, Longaberger Homestead is a salute to small-town America at its best, complete with square dances, children's programs, guided hikes through the countryside, and of course, a wealth of wonderful, freshly prepared food. Here visitors find an incredible array of home-decorating ideas in the Longaberger At Home® shops. You can walk through replicas of J.W. Longaberger's original workshop, nibble tiny sandwiches in an authentic Victorian tea garden, or enjoy a cone in an ice-cream shop named after Dave's imaginary cow he invented for a school project. In the historic Crawford Barn™, you can even make a Longaberger Basket® with your own two hands. Ready to come visit us yourself? To learn more, go to *www.longaberger.com* or call 1-740-322-5588.

BOLOGNESE SAUCE WITH PENNE PASTA

Penne pasta is preferred in this recipe because its large, firm shape holds on nicely to the bits of tomato and ground beef in this traditional Italian sauce. You can also blend the pasta and the sauce together, top it with cheese, and bake it until bubbly.

BOLOGNESE SAUCE WITH PENNE PASTA	From the Longaberger Pantry
2	pounds ripe fresh tomatoes or Italian imported canned tomatoes
1	red onion, finely chopped
2	medium carrots, peeled, finely chopped
2	ribs celery, finely chopped
2	garlic cloves, chopped
1/4	cup chopped fresh parsley
1/4	cup olive oil
1	pound ground chuck
1	cup milk
1/2	cup dry white wine
	Salt and pepper to taste
1/8	teaspoon freshly ground nutmeg
1	pound penne pasta, cooked, drained
	Freshly grated Parmesan cheese

Force the tomatoes through a food mill to purée, discarding the seeds. Sauté the onion, carrots, celery, garlic and parsley in the olive oil in a nonaluminum stockpot until translucent. Add the ground chuck and milk. Cook until the ground chuck is brown, stirring until crumbly. Add the tomato purée, wine, salt, pepper and nutmeg. Simmer for 30 minutes. Adjust the seasonings. Cook for 20 minutes longer. Remove from the heat. Spoon over the hot cooked pasta and sprinkle with the Parmesan cheese.

Serves 6

FRENCH VEAL STEW

Luckily for cooks, the best cuts of veal for stews are also the most economical. And because this veal stew improves with age, it makes a perfect make-ahead entrée.

FRENCH VEAL STEW			From the Longaberger Pantry
1	large yellow onion	2	egg yolks, lightly beaten
4	whole cloves		
2	pounds boned veal shoulder, cut into 1-inch cubes, blanched, drained	1/2	cup heavy cream
		8	ounces button mushrooms, sliced
1	carrot, peeled	1	tablespoon lemon juice
1	rib celery		
1 1/2	teaspoons salt Pepper to taste	12	small white onions, boiled, drained
1/2	teaspoon fines herbes	1/8	teaspoon nutmeg
		1 1/2	to 2 tablespoons lemon juice
1	bay leaf		Salt to taste
2 1/2	cups veal stock or chicken broth	2	teaspoons minced fresh parsley
2	tablespoons butter		
3	tablespoons plus 2 teaspoons flour		

SMART TIP
FINES HERBES

The "fine" in "fines herbes" refers to the way the herbs are chopped in this mixture of equal parts chervil, chives, parsley, and tarragon. Marjoram or savory may also be added to this flavorful blend.

Stud the yellow onion with the cloves. Place the veal, studded onion, carrot, celery, 1 1/2 teaspoons salt, pepper, fines herbes, bay leaf and stock in a large heavy stockpot. Simmer slowly for 1 1/4 to 1 1/2 hours or until the veal is tender. Remove the veal to a bowl with a slotted spoon. Strain the stock mixture and discard the vegetables. Boil in an uncovered saucepan over high heat until reduced to 2 cups.

Melt the butter in a large heavy stockpot over medium heat. Blend in the flour. Stir in the stock gradually. Cook until thickened, stirring constantly. Blend the egg yolks with the cream; stir in a small amount of the hot mixture. Stir into the hot mixture. Toss the mushrooms in 1 tablespoon lemon juice. Add to the stockpot. Cook over medium-low heat for 2 to 3 minutes; do not boil. Add the drained white onions and veal. Cook for 3 to 4 minutes; do not boil. Turn off the heat. Stir in the nutmeg and 1 1/2 to 2 tablespoons lemon juice. Season with salt and pepper to taste. Ladle into a tureen. Sprinkle with the parsley. Serve over buttered noodles.

Serves 6

Spanish Potato Omelet

This is an authentic dish that is prepared often all over Spain. Unlike the familiar rolled omelet that we equate with breakfast here in the States, this omelet is flat and quite thick. Sliced, it is often served as "tapas" (small dishes of food served as appetizers). It's a good recipe to master since it tastes equally good hot, cold, or at room temperature.

SPANISH POTATO OMELET

From the Longaberger Pantry

2	large onions, thinly sliced
4	cups olive oil
6	large potatoes, peeled, thinly sliced (4 pounds)
10	eggs, beaten
1/4	cup chopped fresh parsley
	Salt and pepper to taste

Sauté the onions in the olive oil in a 10-inch nonstick skillet over low heat for 12 minutes or until translucent. Add the potatoes. Cook for 20 minutes or until tender. Remove the onions and potatoes to a colander using a slotted spoon, reserving 1/2 cup of the oil in the skillet.

Season the beaten eggs in a bowl with the parsley, salt and pepper. Fold in the potato mixture gently. Add to the heated reserved oil in the skillet, carefully pushing the mixture down to flatten. Reduce the heat to low. Cook for 12 to 15 minutes or until the bottom is golden brown and set. The omelet should be firm to the touch. Invert a plate over the skillet and carefully flip the omelet onto the plate. Slide the omelet carefully back into the skillet. Cook for 8 to 10 minutes or until set. Invert onto a large serving plate. Cut into wedges.

Serves 6 to 8

Vegetable Wellington

The traditional Beef Wellington is made of beef filet, liver pâté, and buttery pastry. These colorful little bundles are a healthier alternative and make an unconventional vegetarian main course. Or make the packages smaller to serve as appetizers. Freshly prepared vegetables or last-night's leftovers work equally well.

VEGETABLE WELLINGTON

1	bunch asparagus, blanched, cooled, cut into 2-inch pieces
2	carrots, julienned into 2-inch pieces, blanched, cooled
4	ounces snow peas, blanched, cooled, cut into 2-inch strips
1	zucchini, julienned into 2-inch pieces
1	yellow squash, julienned into 2-inch pieces
1	red bell pepper, julienned into 2-inch strips
6	sheets frozen phyllo dough, thawed
1/2	cup (1 stick) butter, melted
1/2	cup Perfect Pesto (page 130), or purchased pesto
1/4	cup chopped fresh basil
1/4	cup chopped fresh parsley

Arrange a mixture of the vegetables in 6 to 8 individual bundles. Pat the vegetables dry with paper towels.

Unroll the dough and cover with a damp towel to keep moist. Place 1 sheet of dough on a cutting board. Brush with butter. Place another sheet on top and brush with butter. Top with a third sheet and brush with 1/4 cup of the Perfect Pesto. Cut the stacked sheets horizontally into thirds or quarters. Place 1 bundle of vegetables at an angle 2 inches from the top. Fold 1 corner across the vegetables and continue to fold as for a flag. Tuck the excess dough under. Repeat the process until all packages are assembled. Place the triangles on a nonstick baking sheet. Brush the tops with butter. Sprinkle with the basil and parsley. Bake at 350 degrees for 20 to 25 minutes or until golden brown. Serve whole or cut into halves diagonally with your favorite tomato sauce.

Serves 6 to 8

Choosing Sides?

Just when you've finally answered the question: "What's for dinner?" the question of side dishes crops up. How does a creative cook choose? After considering what seemed like all of America's current favorites, we started choosing sides for this book by looking inside our own pantries for familiar staples, like pasta, bread, rice, and potatoes, that we all rely on to fill out our family's meals. Then we chose a variety of always-available vegetables—fresh carrots and zucchini and green beans come to mind—that are bold in flavor and nutrient-rich. From there, knowing that simple techniques keep nutrients intact, we combined the staples and vegetables into recipes that aren't overly complicated, relying instead on the vegetables' just-picked flavors, lively textures, and vibrant colors to keep each dish interesting. Finally, we found that improvising made everything new again. (You will, too.)

HOW ABOUT POTATOES?

Did you know that the average American consumes fourteen ten-pound bags of potatoes a year? We say, if we're all eating that many, we'd better make them interesting! We've come up with a few ways, but we also think there's nothing better than a plain baked potato drizzled with extra-virgin olive oil and sprinkled with sea salt and pepper—proof that a few simple, fresh ingredients can be as delicious as some fancy creation that takes hours to make.

The potato has been a central feature in European and American diets for hundreds of years. Popular with the Inca tribes of Peru who developed more than two hundred varieties, the equally impressed Spanish conquistadors brought potatoes back home to Europe in the sixteenth century. There the potato was slow to catch on because most people recognized it as a member of the poisonous nightshade plant family. Frederick the Great, the Prussian ruler, ordered his people to plant and eat potatoes as a deterrent to famine. His people's fear of poisoning persisted until he threatened to cut off the nose and ears of those who refused. Not surprisingly, this was effective, and one generation later, potatoes were a staple of the Prussian masses!

Today more than one hundred varieties of this humble vegetable are cultivated, in colors ranging from creamy white to blue, purple, yellow, and red. Store yours in a dark, well-ventilated place at room temperature. Refrigerated potatoes convert their starch to sugar, resulting in soft, wrinkled skins, mealiness, and flavor loss. Potatoes exposed to light will turn green and sprout. Don't store potatoes with onions, either; they exchange gases and speed up the deterioration of both.

Potatoes fall into two basic types—boilers and bakers. Waxy boilers are best for salads, since they hold their shape best. Starchy bakers cook up dry and fluffy, so they're just right for baking, frying, and mashing. Many dishes prepared with regular potatoes can also be made with sweet potatoes or yams. Sweet potatoes, however, have a shorter shelf life and should be used within ten days.

ROASTED FRENCH POTATO SALAD WITH BACON

Since this version of the much-loved classic contains no mayo or eggs, you can serve it at room temperature indoors or out. Consider making a meal of salads: Toss shredded leftover chicken in fresh lemon juice, olive oil, salt, black pepper, and red pepper flakes. Toss again with coarsely chopped Italian parsley and toasted pine nuts. Serve on a bed of fresh greens alongside French Potato Salad.

FRENCH POTATO SALAD WITH BACON

From the Longaberger Pantry

1	pound new potatoes	2	tablespoons olive oil
4	ounces bacon, chopped		Salt and pepper to taste
1/4	cup finely chopped shallots	1/4	cup chopped purple onion
1/4	cup red wine vinegar	1/2	cup chopped parsley

Scrub the potatoes under running water with a soft brush. Cut the potatoes into quarters and place on a foil-lined baking sheet. Roast at 350 degrees for 15 to 20 minutes or until tender but still firm.

Sauté the bacon in a small skillet until crisp. Remove the bacon, reserving 1/3 cup of the drippings in the skillet. Crumble the bacon and reserve for the topping. Add the shallots to the skillet. Sauté for 5 minutes or until tender but not brown.

Place the hot potatoes in a bowl. Add the vinegar, olive oil, undrained shallots, salt and pepper and toss gently to mix. Add the purple onion and parsley and toss again. Cool to room temperature. Chill, covered, in the refrigerator. Return to room temperature before serving. Adjust the seasonings to taste and add additional olive oil and vinegar if needed. Sprinkle with the reserved bacon.

Serves 4

SMART TIP

BET YOU DIDN'T KNOW...

...that you should cook potatoes with as much of their skin on as possible. Cooking potatoes in their skins keeps them from absorbing water, which leaches flavor and nutrients.
...that you should use the water in which potatoes are steamed or boiled, for gravy or for moistening mashed potatoes. It's full of vitamins.
...that you should never bake potatoes in aluminum foil. Foil seals in the moisture and steams the potato, making it pasty instead of dry and fluffy.
...that if you use metal skewers to cut the baking time of potatoes, you should heat the skewers first to prevent centers from darkening.
...that real potato connoisseurs never open a baked potato with a knife. Instead, they poke a zigzag pattern across the top of the potato, then press the sides together to make the inside "blossom."

POTATO WEDGES WITH PARMESAN

From the Longaberger Pantry

5	pounds Yukon potatoes		Dash of cayenne
2	tablespoons olive oil		pepper, paprika and
1/4	cup grated Parmesan cheese		chili powder
	Chopped fresh herbs		Salt and black pepper
	to taste		to taste

Peel the potatoes and cut each lengthwise into 6 wedges. Toss the potatoes with the olive oil, Parmesan cheese, herbs, cayenne pepper, paprika, chili powder, salt and black pepper in a bowl. Arrange in a single layer in an oiled large shallow baking pan. Bake at 425 degrees for 40 minutes or until the undersides are golden brown. Turn the potatoes over. Bake for 20 minutes longer or until golden brown and tender.
   Serves 8

NEW POTATOES WITH DILL AND LEMON

From the Longaberger Pantry

5	tablespoons unsalted	2	teaspoons
	butter, melted		kosher salt,
2 1/2	pounds whole new		or to taste
	potatoes, scrubbed		Pepper to taste
2	tablespoons fresh dill		Zest of 1 lemon

Pour 1/2 of the butter into an 8-inch baking dish, being sure to coat the bottom. Place the potatoes in the prepared dish. Sprinkle with the dill, kosher salt, pepper and lemon zest. Pour the remaining butter over the potatoes. Place on the middle oven rack. Bake at 425 degrees for 45 to 60 minutes or until crisp and golden brown. Sprinkle the potatoes with additional dill, kosher salt and lemon zest if desired.
   Serves 4

SPICY CUMIN SWEET POTATOES

From the Longaberger Pantry

3	tablespoons	1 1/2	pounds sweet
	unsalted butter		potatoes, peeled,
1	teaspoon cumin		cut into 1-inch pieces
	Salt and pepper to taste		(about 2 cups)

Melt the butter in a small saucepan. Stir in the cumin, salt and pepper. Place the sweet potatoes in a small baking pan. Add the butter mixture and toss to coat. Bake at 450 degrees for 15 to 20 minutes or until golden brown and tender.
   Serves 4

Mashed Roasted Sweet Potatoes

Uh-oh. Sweet potatoes ready before the rest of the meal? Keep them warm in a double boiler. Or put them in one of our buttered pottery Baking Dishes, float a thin layer of cream on top, cover the dish with plastic wrap, and place in a warm (not hot) oven. And relax, okay?

MASHED ROASTED SWEET POTATOES

From the
Longaberger
Pantry

3	pounds sweet potatoes
2	tablespoons olive oil
1/4	cup (1/2 stick) unsalted butter
	Juice of 1 lime
	Sea salt to taste
1/4	teaspoon cayenne pepper

Scrub the sweet potatoes and pat dry. Place in a large bowl. Add the olive oil and toss to coat. Pierce a few holes in the sweet potatoes. Place on a baking sheet. Bake at 375 degrees for 30 to 40 minutes or until the sweet potatoes are soft. Cool slightly.

Peel the sweet potatoes and place in a large mixing bowl. Add the butter and lime juice and mash until smooth. Season with sea salt and cayenne pepper.

Serves 6 to 8

V A R I A T I O N

For *Mashed Bleu Cheese Potatoes,* substitute Yukon Gold potatoes or round white potatoes for the sweet potatoes, and substitute 4 ounces bleu cheese for the lime juice. Add 3/4 cup buttermilk and 2 scallions, chopped.

GLAZED CARROTS

Use medium to small organic carrots, if possible, for this recipe. For a snazzy touch, slice carrots at an angle.

VARIATION

For **Mashed Rutabaga Carrots,** peel 1/2 of a rutabaga and cut into 1-inch pieces. Cook with the carrots until both are soft. Mash coarsely with a potato masher and adjust the seasonings to taste.

GLAZED CARROTS

From the Longaberger Pantry

6	medium or small carrots, thinly sliced	2	tablespoons brown sugar
1/4	cup water	2	tablespoons butter
1	tablespoon butter	1	teaspoon balsamic vinegar
	Salt to taste		

Place the carrots, water, 1 tablespoon butter and salt in a saucepan. Cover tightly to lock in the aroma of the carrots. Simmer over low heat for 15 to 20 minutes or until tender-crisp and the carrots have absorbed the water. Combine the brown sugar, 2 tablespoons butter and vinegar in a saucepan. Cook until well blended. Pour immediately over the carrots and toss to coat.

Serves 4

SWISS CHARD WITH MUSHROOMS

Swiss chard is available in three colors: red, white, and yellow. Take your pick for this recipe, rejoicing in Swiss chard's low-calorie and high-calcium content (1/2 cup is about 90 mgs).

SWISS CHARD WITH MUSHROOMS

From the Longaberger Pantry

1 1/2	pounds Swiss chard	1/4	cup water, chicken stock or vegetable stock
1	tablespoon butter		
1	tablespoon olive oil		
2	small shallots, minced		Salt and pepper to taste
1	pound fresh button mushrooms, sliced		

Trim the chard and separate the leaves from the stems. Cut the chard stems into 1-inch pieces and the leaves into smaller pieces. Heat the butter and olive oil in a saucepan over medium heat. Stir in the shallots. Cook until slightly softened. Add the mushrooms. Cook until tender. Add the chard stems and water or stock. Simmer, covered, for 10 minutes or until tender. (The timing may vary, so check often.) Add the chard leaves. Simmer, covered, until tender. Uncover and increase the heat. Cook until some of the liquid has evaporated. Season with salt and pepper. Next time use spinach instead of the Swiss chard.

Serves 2 or 3

GREEN BEAN SAUTÉ

There's a saying that "You eat with your eyes." A pile of these vibrant, glistening green beans on our plates satisfies our eyes very much indeed. Although today's fresh green beans aren't as tough as they used to be, it's still a good idea to string them before cooking.

GREEN BEAN SAUTÉ		From the Longaberger Pantry
4	cups water	
	Salt to taste	
1	pound snapped fresh green beans	
1/4	cup olive oil or sesame oil	
1/4	teaspoon salt	
1	tablespoon lemon juice	
1	tablespoon grated lemon zest	
2	garlic cloves, cut into slivers	

Bring the water and salt to taste to a boil in a saucepan and reduce the heat to medium. Add the green beans. Cook, covered, for 10 minutes or until tender; drain.

Pour the olive oil into a saucepan. Add 1/4 teaspoon salt, lemon juice, lemon zest and garlic. Sauté over medium heat for 2 to 3 minutes or until heated through (do not let the garlic take on color). Arrange the green beans on a serving platter. Drizzle with the garlic mixture.

Serves 4

VARIATIONS

For *Broccoli Sauté,* use 1 bunch of broccoli instead of the green beans.

For *Zucchini and Yellow Squash with Red Pepper Strips,* substitute 3 zucchini, 1 yellow squash and 1 red bell pepper for the green beans. Rinse the zucchini and yellow squash. Cut the squash into strips with a vegetable peeler until you hit the seeds. (The strips will resemble noodles.) Cut the bell pepper into julienne strips.

JICAMA SLAW

Jicama (pronounced "hick-a-ma") is often referred to as a Mexican potato. Native to Central and South America, it's a root that tastes somewhat like a water chestnut. Since it holds its mild flavor and crunch so well, try jicama uncooked in salads. For a change-of-pace snack, cut it into sticks for dipping into a spicy salsa. Scrub jicama well, then use a sharp paring knife to peel it—the thin skin pulls right off.

PREPARATION TIP
MAKE A CABBAGE BED

Any of the slaws here make interesting contrasts to grilled fish. Next time, place the catch of the day atop a thick bed of slaw. Squeeze fresh lime juice over the fish. Finish with a sprinkle of salt, pepper and paprika.

JICAMA SLAW

1	medium head green cabbage, shredded
1/4	head red cabbage, shredded
1	carrot, cut into julienne strips
1	red bell pepper, chopped
6	green onions, sliced
1/2	cup chopped fresh cilantro
1/2	cup chopped fresh parsley
1	medium jicama, cut into julienne strips
1/3	cup vegetable oil
1/3	cup lime juice
1/3	cup orange juice
1	tablespoon chopped canned chipotle chiles
1	teaspoon ground coriander
1	teaspoon ground cumin
	Dash of freshly ground pepper

Toss the green cabbage, red cabbage, carrot, bell pepper, green onions, cilantro, parsley and jicama in a large bowl. Mix the oil, lime juice, orange juice, chiles, coriander, cumin and pepper in a bowl until blended. Add to the cabbage mixture and toss to mix well. Chill, covered, for 2 hours before serving.

Serves 8

VARIATIONS

For *Celery Slaw*, substitute julienne of celery for the jicama, substitute 1 tablespoon chopped ginger for the chiles and add 1 tablespoon sesame oil with the remaining ingredients. Garnish with cilantro leaves and lime wedges.

For *Cabbage Slaw,* substitute 1/2 medium head green cabbage and 1/2 medium head red cabbage, shredded, for the jicama, and add the remaining ingredients.

Oven-Roasted Vegetables With Balsamic Vinegar

The olive oil in this recipe keeps these veggies moist, while salt draws out their most intense flavors. Serve hot, at room temperature, or cold as a charming, chunky salad.

VEGETABLES WITH BALSAMIC VINEGAR

From the
Longaberger
Pantry

1/2	cup olive oil
1	pound eggplant, cut crosswise into slices 1/3 inch thick
1 1/4	pounds zucchini, cut crosswise into slices 1/3 inch thick
4	large plum tomatoes (about 1 1/4 pounds), cut lengthwise into slices 1/3 inch thick
2	medium red onions, cut into slices 1/3 inch thick
1	pound medium red potatoes, cut into slices 1/3 inch thick
	Salt and pepper to taste
1	tablespoon balsamic vinegar

Brush 2 baking sheets with some of the olive oil. Arrange as many of the vegetables as possible in a single layer on the prepared baking sheets. Brush the vegetables with some of the remaining olive oil. Season with salt and pepper. Place the baking sheets on the middle and lower third oven racks. Roast at 450 degrees for 10 to 15 minutes or until tender and light brown, switching the positions of the baking sheets in the oven halfway through the roasting time. Arrange the roasted vegetables in a single layer in our 9×13-inch Baking Dish. Repeat the process with the remaining vegetables. Toss the roasted vegetables with the balsamic vinegar just before serving.

Serves 6 to 8

Do-Ahead Tip
ROAST IN ADVANCE

You may roast the vegetables 1 day ahead of time. Cool completely and layer on a tray between sheets of plastic wrap. Cover and chill in the refrigerator. Bring vegetables to room temperature before serving.

GRILLED CORN ON THE COB WITH FETA

If you think there's nothing tastier than a fresh ear of corn from a stand on the county fair midway, you're probably right. On the other hand, you've probably never tried it like this, with mayonnaise, lime juice, cayenne pepper, and crumbled feta cheese. You'll love it!

GRILLED CORN ON THE COB WITH FETA

From the Longaberger Pantry

4	ears of corn in the husk
1/4	cup mayonnaise
1	tablespoon lime juice
1/8	teaspoon cayenne pepper, or to taste
3/4	cup crumbled feta cheese

Soak the corn in the husks in cold water in a large pan for 10 minutes; drain. Place the corn on a grill rack set 5 to 6 inches above glowing coals. Grill for 10 minutes or until the husks are charred. Pull back the husks, exposing the corn kernels and return to the grill rack. Grill for 10 minutes or until the kernels are brown in spots.

Whisk the mayonnaise, lime juice and cayenne pepper in a small bowl. Brush over the hot corn and sprinkle with the feta cheese.

Serves 4

PREPARATION TIP
OVEN-ROASTED CORN ON THE COB

Can you get fresh-roasted corn flavor in the cold winter months? Yes! Preheat your oven to 350 degrees. Soak the corn in the husks in cold water in a large pan for 10 minutes. The moisture is important to prevent the corn from drying out. Drain the corn. Place the corn directly on the middle oven rack. Bake for 15 to 20 minutes. Pull back the husks and serve as above.

ZUCCHINI PANCAKES

Do friends walk the other way when they see you coming with armloads of zucchini from your garden? Share this recipe and they'll accept your zucchini gracefully. This dish makes a sure-fire first course, or try it snuggled up to almost any weekday roast.

From the
Longaberger
Pantry

ZUCCHINI PANCAKES

2	large zucchini, grated (about 3 cups)
2	eggs, beaten
1/4	cup fresh Italian parsley, chopped
2	tablespoons chopped shallot
3	tablespoons flour
3/4	teaspoon sea salt
1/4	teaspoon fresh cracked pepper
2	tablespoons vegetable oil
1	cup salsa, or 1/4 cup grated Parmesan cheese

Combine the zucchini, eggs, parsley, shallot, flour, sea salt and pepper in a bowl and mix well. Heat 1 tablespoon of the vegetable oil in a nonstick skillet over medium heat. Drop the zucchini mixture 2 tablespoons at a time into the hot oil, flattening each pancake slightly and adding the remaining oil as needed between batches. Fry for 2 to 3 minutes on each side or until set. Place on a broiler pan. Broil for 1 to 2 minutes or until golden brown and crispy. Serve with salsa or a sprinkling of Parmesan cheese.

Makes 16 pancakes

V A R I A T I O N

For *Potato Pancakes,* substitute 3 cups shredded potatoes, rinsed and dried, for the zucchini and eliminate 1 egg. Serve with sour cream and caviar, or to kids with sour cream and applesauce. (Note: Be sure to soak the shredded potatoes in water, changing the water several times to remove some of the starch. Dry the potatoes thoroughly before adding the remaining ingredients.)

BAKED MACARONI AND CHEESE

Originating in the early part of the nineteenth century, macaroni and cheese is the quintessential comfort food and the undisputed choice of hungry American children. The toasted bread crumbs in this recipe add a crunchy contrast to the rich, creamy cheese and soft noodles. Assemble it up to a day ahead, but bake it just before serving.

CHANGE THE CHEESE, PLEASE

To change the personality of your mac 'n' cheese, simply substitute different kinds of cheese. We like a combination of mild and sharp cheeses, but if your family prefers a creamier, milder flavor, stick with American cheese. For the biggest cheese taste, combine classic New York and Wisconsin Cheddar cheeses.

BAKED MACARONI AND CHEESE

1 1/2	cups uncooked macaroni
	Salt to taste
1	cup fresh bread crumbs
1/2	cup grated Parmesan cheese
2	tablespoons unsalted butter, melted
1	pound sharp Cheddar cheese
1/4	cup (1/2 stick) butter, melted
2	eggs, beaten
1	cup milk
	Pepper to taste

Cook the macaroni in boiling salted water in a medium saucepan until just tender. Do not overcook.

Combine the bread crumbs, Parmesan cheese and 2 tablespoons unsalted butter in a bowl and mix well. (Note: We like crumbs made from French bread, but any bread crumbs, or even saltine crackers, will do. If you omit the Parmesan cheese, add a pinch of salt.)

Shred the Cheddar cheese and reserve 1/2 cup for the topping. Drain the macaroni and return to the saucepan. Add 1/4 cup butter and the remaining Cheddar cheese and mix well. Add the eggs and mix well. Stir in the milk, salt and pepper. Cook over medium heat for 3 minutes, stirring constantly. Grease our 8×8-inch Baking Dish or 2-Quart Covered Casserole. Pour in the macaroni mixture. Sprinkle with the reserved Cheddar cheese. Bake at 350 degrees for 10 minutes. Remove from the oven and stir. Top with the bread crumb mixture. Bake for 15 minutes longer.

Serves 8

Help with Lunch and Snacks

Sometimes, pouring breakfast cereal and picking up dinner on the way home is the most you can manage in one day. That leaves anyone in need of lunch or a snack to fend for themselves. If you prefer that those lunches and snacks consist of something other than diet colas and red licorice, take action beforehand. Set up a Lunch Maker's Basket using our versatile Hostess Serving Tray. Just slip in it's clever plastic divided protector, then place a stack of brown paper lunch bags in the center compartment. Stock the remaining compartments with mini cans of fruit, packages of peanut butter and crackers, and spare change for milk money. Alternatively, turn our beautifully hand-crafted Gathering Basket into a Snack Attack Center, with granola bars, unsalted almonds, individually wrapped rice cakes, shiny apples, and juice boxes at the ready.

It's a simple way to do something nice for everybody who comes into your kitchen. Like our founder Dave Longaberger always used to say: "Do something that's good for a lot of people, and two things will happen. You'll have fun and your day will instantly be better."

FETTUCCINI ALFREDO

A side of this classic creamy pasta will always draw raves, but for fans who can never get enough, remember that an entrée of Fettuccini Alfredo can be prepared in about 30 minutes.

BETTER-FOR-YOU FETTUCCINI ALFREDO

For **Better-For-You Fettuccini Alfredo,** *melt 2 tablespoons butter in a medium saucepan. Stir in 2 tablespoons flour. Cook for 1 minute. Add 1½ cups 1% milk and ½ cup cream and whisk until smooth. Add ¼ teaspoon freshly grated nutmeg, a pinch of salt and a few grinds of pepper. Cook until thick and creamy, stirring constantly. Pour over the hot fettuccini in a large bowl. Add 2 cups grated Parmesan cheese, ¼ cup chopped fresh basil and ¼ cup chopped fresh Italian parsley and toss to coat. Season with salt and pepper to taste.*

FETTUCCINI ALFREDO	From the Longaberger Pantry
½	cup (1 stick) butter or margarine, softened
2	cups heavy cream
1	to 2 cups grated Parmesan cheese
12	ounces fettuccini
¼	cup chopped fresh basil, or 1½ tablespoons dried basil
	Freshly ground pepper to taste

Combine the butter, cream and Parmesan cheese in a large bowl and mix until blended. Cook the pasta using the package directions; drain well. Add the hot pasta to the cheese mixture and toss until coated. Spoon onto a warm serving platter. Sprinkle with the basil and pepper.

Serves 4

VARIATIONS

For *Grilled Chicken Fettuccini Alfredo,* grill and slice 4 chicken breasts and toss with the pasta above.

For *Smoked Salmon Fettuccini Alfredo,* add 6 ounces cooked frozen peas, 6 ounces blanched snow peas, and 6 ounces smoked salmon, cut into julienne strips. Add to the pasta above.

For *Fettuccini Alfredo Primavera,* cut up and steam 1 pound of your favorite vegetables and add to the pasta above.

For *Grilled Shrimp Fettuccini,* grill 2 pounds of marinated peeled shrimp and sauté 1 pound of sugar snap peas. Toss both with the pasta above.

TOMATO SAUCE WITH SPAGHETTI

We admit it. We fall back on the occasional jar of grocery-store spaghetti sauce every now and then. But when we grow wistful for the full, vibrant flavors of mom's homemade spaghetti sauce, we turn to this recipe. It's surprisingly easy. But since you're going to the trouble anyway, why not make a big batch and freeze it in smaller quantities? You'll feel smug for months.

TOMATO SAUCE WITH SPAGHETTI

From the Longaberger Pantry

1/4	cup extra-virgin olive oil	1	(28-ounce) can Italian plum tomatoes
1	cup chopped red onion		
2	garlic cloves, finely chopped	2	ounces sun-dried tomatoes, chopped
2	tablespoons capers	1/4	cup red wine
1/2	teaspoon red pepper flakes		Salt and black pepper to taste
1	teaspoon each oregano and basil	16	ounces spaghetti, cooked, drained

Combine the olive oil, onion, garlic, capers, red pepper flakes, oregano and basil in a large ovenproof pan. Simmer for 3 to 4 minutes, stirring constantly. Add the plum tomatoes, sun-dried tomatoes, red wine, salt and black pepper. Roast at 450 degrees for 15 to 20 minutes or until brown. Spoon the sauce over the hot pasta.

Serves 4 to 6

GREEK BOW TIE PASTA

Even if no one at home is vegetarian, we all know there are all kinds of good reasons to make a meatless meal now and then. Suffice it to say that, with a tossed green salad and a few hunks of Pesto Garlic Bread (facing page), this pasta dish makes a memorable meal.

GREEK BOW TIE PASTA

From the Longaberger Pantry

4	garlic cloves, minced	1	cup fresh Italian parsley
1/3	cup olive oil		
1/4	cup kalamata olives, pitted, cut into halves		Salt and pepper to taste
1	(6-ounce) jar roasted red peppers, cut into strips	1/2	cup crumbled feta cheese
		16	ounces bow tie pasta

Sauté the garlic in the olive oil in a skillet. Cook for just a few minutes. Remove from the heat. Combine with the olives, red peppers, parsley, salt and pepper in a large ceramic bowl and mix well. Cook and drain pasta. Add pasta to sauce and toss to coat. Sprinkle with the feta cheese and fold into the pasta. Serve immediately.

Serves 4 to 6

PESTO GARLIC BREAD

From the
Longaberger
Pantry

1	loaf Italian or French bread, split, quartered
1/2	cup olive oil
1	cup Perfect Pesto (page 130)
2	garlic cloves, chopped
1	cup grated Parmesan cheese

Place the bread cut side up on a foil-lined baking sheet. Brush with olive oil. Mix the Perfect Pesto and garlic in a bowl. Spread 1/4 cup of the mixture on each piece of bread. Sprinkle with the cheese. Bake at 350 degrees for 15 minutes or until golden brown. Cut into slices to serve.

Serves 4 to 6

PENNE WITH PERFECT PESTO

You'll be sorely disappointed if you use dried herbs in this pesto recipe, but feel free to vary the shape of the pasta. Serve the penne hot or at room temperature. Add grilled shrimp to make it a main dish. Our pesto recipe makes more than enough for this pasta dish, so plan on spreading what is left over onto toasted French bread. Or throw a tablespoon or two into a pot of homemade minestrone for authenticity.

VARIATIONS

For *Arugula Pesto,* substitute arugula leaves for the basil leaves for a vivid peppery taste. Either pesto is fabulous brushed on grilled shrimp and scallops hot off the grill.

For out-of-this-world grilled chicken sandwiches, spread pesto on French bread and top with slices of grilled chicken and provolone cheese. Serve the sandwiches at room temperature or warmed in the oven.

PENNE WITH PERFECT PESTO

From the Longaberger Pantry

4	quarts water
1 1/2	tablespoons salt
16	ounces penne pasta
1/3	cup heavy cream
1	cup Perfect Pesto (below)
	Freshly ground pepper to taste
	Freshly grated imported Parmesan or Romano cheese (optional)

Bring the water to a boil in a large kettle or stockpot. Add the salt and return to a boil. Add the pasta, stirring with a wooden fork or spoon until submerged. Boil for 12 minutes or until al dente (cooked only until the pasta gives a slight resistance when bitten into). Drain, reserving 2 tablespoons of the water. Return the hot pasta to the stockpot. Combine the reserved water, cream and Perfect Pesto in a bowl and mix well. Add to the pasta and toss to coat. Serve immediately on warm plates. Sprinkle with freshly ground pepper and Parmesan cheese if desired.

Serves 6

PERFECT PESTO

From the Longaberger Pantry

2	cups fresh basil leaves, rinsed, patted dry
4	medium garlic cloves, peeled, chopped
1	cup walnuts or pine nuts, toasted
1	cup olive oil
1	cup freshly grated Parmesan cheese
	Salt and freshly ground pepper to taste

Combine the basil, garlic and walnuts in a food processor container. Process until chopped. Add the olive oil in a fine steady stream, processing constantly. Add the Parmesan cheese, salt and pepper. Process briefly until combined. Scrape into a bowl and store, covered, in the refrigerator until ready to use. For a bold, jewel-toned pesto, add 1/2 cup Italian parsley leaves to the fresh basil leaves.

Makes 2 cups

DO-AHEAD TIP
PESTO, PRESTO

In the summer months, when gardens are overflowing with basil and Italian parsley, prepare a large batch of pesto and freeze it in ice cube trays. Once it's frozen, pop the cubes out and tumble them into a freezer bag. They'll keep for several months in your freezer. Thaw as many cubes as you need, as you need them.

COLD RICE AND VEGETABLE SALAD

When we take bowls of this colorful salad to potluck suppers, our bowls come up empty first. Need we say more?

COLD RICE AND VEGETABLE SALAD

From the Longaberger Pantry

1¹/3	cups uncooked long grain rice
1/3	cup lemon juice
2/3	cup olive oil
1	tablespoon minced green onions
1/2	teaspoon salt
	Dash of pepper
1/2	to 1 teaspoon curry powder
1/2	teaspoon dry mustard
1/4	cup chopped fresh parsley
3/4	cup chopped cooked chicken (optional)
1	cup fresh cauliflower florets
1	cup frozen green peas, cooked, chilled
1/2	cup chopped celery
1/2	cup sliced radishes
	Romaine

Cook the rice using the package directions. Add the lemon juice and olive oil and toss lightly. Spoon into a large salad bowl. Chill, covered, for several hours.

Combine the green onions, 1/2 teaspoon salt, pepper, curry powder, dry mustard and parsley in a bowl and mix well. Add to the chilled rice and toss to mix. Add the chicken, cauliflower, peas, celery and radishes and toss lightly. Serve on romaine-lined serving plates.

(Note: The easiest way to cook rice without undercooking or burning it is to boil in a large saucepan of salted water like pasta. Drain the rice, shake off the excess water and return to the saucepan over heat. Fluff the rice with a fork to help evaporate any remaining moisture.)

Serves 6 to 8

HEALTHY TIP
RICE FOR UPSET TUMMIES

We don't know why, but this homemade remedy for upset tummies always seems to work for us: Cook 1 cup of long grain rice in 3 cups of water for 15 minutes. Strain the cooked rice from the liquid, reserving both. Cool the liquid and serve in a mug. (You can sweeten it with a pinch of sugar if you'd like.) Use the reserved rice for this cold rice salad or a lovely rice pudding.

RICE PILAF

Why serve plain old white rice when you can serve a beautiful pilaf with not much more work? This one adds drama to grilled or roasted meats and fish. Other pilafs, (below right), require only a few more ingredients.

From the Longaberger Pantry

RICE PILAF

1/4	cup (1/2 stick) unsalted butter
2 1/2	cups chopped onions
1	cup uncooked basmati rice
2	medium garlic cloves, minced
2	cups chicken or vegetable stock
	Salt and freshly ground pepper to taste
3	tablespoons chopped fresh parsley

Melt the butter in a heavy Dutch oven or enamel cast-iron dish. Add the onions. Sauté for 20 minutes or until translucent. Add the rice. Sauté for 1 minute or until the rice is coated. Add the garlic, chicken stock, salt and pepper. Bring to a boil, stirring constantly. Reduce the heat. Simmer, covered, for 20 minutes or until the liquid is absorbed. Remove from the heat. Let stand for 5 minutes to steam. Uncover and fluff the rice. Adjust the seasonings. Stir in the parsley.

Serves 4 to 6

SMART TIP
WHY BASMATI?

Any kind of rice can be used in any of the pilafs (at right). But we like basmati rice best. It has a nutty fragrance and gives pilafs their irresistible fluffiness. Some of the starch in basmati needs to be removed or the grains will stick together as they cook. Just soak the rice in a bath of cold water for 3 minutes; strain and repeat the process twice.

VARIATIONS

- Add 1 garlic clove, minced, with the chopped onions.
- Add a pinch of saffron to the boiling water before you cook the rice.
- For *Jeweled Rice* (pictured on facing page), add chopped dates, pistachios and chopped parsley to the saffron rice variation.
- Add 2 tablespoons lemon juice, 1 teaspoon lemon zest, 2 tablespoons grated Parmesan cheese and an additional 2 tablespoons chopped fresh parsley.
- Substitute coconut milk for 1/2 of the cooking liquid.
- Add 1/4 cup Perfect Pesto (page 130) and 1/2 cup grated Parmesan cheese to cooked rice.
- Add 1/2 cup each of corn kernels and green peas to cooked rice (pictured on facing page).
- Add 1/2 cup currants, toasted pine nuts and chopped parsley to cooked rice.

MICROWAVE WILD MUSHROOM RISOTTO

Risotto is the premier dish of Verona, Italy. There it's prepared in the traditional way, on the stove top, stirred constantly while hot liquid is added to create a creamy texture and a distinctive bite. Since we're not fond of standing over a hot burner, stirring and stirring and stirring, we like this risotto because it can be prepared in the microwave. We show it here in our pottery Covered Casserole Dish.

MICROWAVE WILD MUSHROOM RISOTTO

From the
Longaberger
Pantry

1	ounce dried wild mushrooms, preferably porcini, well rinsed
2/3	cup water
1	small onion, chopped
1	garlic clove, minced (optional)
3	tablespoons olive oil
1	cup uncooked arborio rice
2	cups chicken broth
1/2	cup grated Parmesan cheese
	Chopped fresh parsley for garnish

Soak the dried mushrooms in the water for 15 minutes. Drain the mushrooms, reserving the liquid. Rinse the mushrooms again in running water and pat dry with paper towels. Combine the mushrooms, onion, garlic and olive oil in a microwave-safe dish. Microwave, covered, on High for 1 to 2 minutes or until the onion is tender. Stir in the rice. Add the chicken broth and reserved liquid. Microwave, covered, on High for 5 to 6 minutes or until the broth begins to boil. Microwave on Medium for 20 minutes or until most of the liquid is absorbed. Stir in the Parmesan cheese. Let stand for 5 minutes before serving. Garnish with chopped parsley.

Serves 4

VARIATIONS

For the following variations, omit the mushrooms in the recipe above.

For *Risotto Milanese,* stir 1/4 teaspoon saffron threads into the broth. Add the remaining ingredients.

For *Risotto with Pesto,* stir 1/2 cup Perfect Pesto (page 130) into the cooked risotto or use store-bought pesto with 1/4 cup chopped fresh parsley. Sprinkle with additional grated Parmesan cheese.

For *Risotto con Piselli Verdi* (with green peas), place 8 ounces of frozen green peas in a bowl covered with plastic wrap while the risotto is being microwaved. As soon as the risotto is finished, remove from the oven and microwave the peas until hot. Mash 1/3 of the peas and stir into the risotto with the remaining whole peas. Adjust the seasonings and sprinkle with additional grated Parmesan cheese.

136

PUMPKIN BREAD

This sweet and spicy loaf is a quick bread, which means it can be ready for the oven in a matter of minutes. The recipe suggests that you pour the batter into two of our Loaf Dishes, but you can generally bake quick breads in any shape or size of ovenproof container. Try baking quick breads in our pottery Flower Pots or Crocks, or your own muffin cups. Just bake until a wooden pick poked in the center comes out clean.

STORAGE TIP

LEFTOVER PUMPKIN PURÉE?

If your family likes Pumpkin Bread (and whose doesn't?), they'll also probably like pumpkin cheesecake or pumpkin pancakes. So for future recipes, store leftover pumpkin purée in an airtight plastic food storage bag in the freezer for up to 3 months. Don't forget to label and date the package.

PUMPKIN BREAD

From the Longaberger Pantry

1³/4	cups flour
1/2	cup packed light brown sugar
1	teaspoon baking soda
1/2	teaspoon salt
2	teaspoons ground ginger
1	teaspoon ground cinnamon
1/2	teaspoon ground allspice
1/2	teaspoon ground nutmeg
3	ounces unsalted butter, chilled, cut into 1-inch pieces
2	large eggs, beaten
1/2	cup maple syrup
1	cup pumpkin purée
1/2	cup golden raisins, plumped
1/2	cup toasted pecans, chopped

Butter 2 of our Loaf Dishes. Mix the flour, brown sugar, baking soda, salt, ginger, cinnamon, allspice and nutmeg in a mixing bowl or food processor. Cut in the butter until it resembles cornmeal. Combine the eggs, maple syrup and pumpkin purée in a bowl and mix well. Add to the flour mixture. Beat at low speed for about 30 seconds or until blended. Fold in the golden raisins and toasted pecans gently. Do not overmix. Pour into the prepared Loaf Dishes. Bake at 325 degrees for 45 to 50 minutes or until a wooden pick inserted in the center comes out clean. Cool in the pans for 20 minutes or longer. Invert to unmold the loaves. Serve with butter, cream cheese or with cinnamon ice cream for dessert.

Makes 2 loaves

VARIATION

Out of pumpkin purée? Make **Sweet Potato Bread** instead! The same quantity of cooked and mashed sweet potatoes can be substituted for pumpkin. The sweet potatoes will produce a sweet and moist bread. Plumped dried cranberries can be added to the bread. Soak 1/2 cup of dried cranberries in warm water for 5 minutes; drain. Add to the batter.

FOCACCIA

Don't let the fancy Italian name scare you—focaccia is basically a pizza. More bread, fewer toppings. Like pizza dough, it's made from yeast, but don't let that intimidate you either, because focaccia is a snap to make (note how few ingredients). Plus everyone loves the smell as it bakes. We've provided a variety of toppings to try, but don't overlook the simple charm of shaved fresh Parmesan cheese, a sprinkle of sea salt, and a swipe of olive oil, especially if you're rushed.

FOCACCIA

From the
Longaberger
Pantry

1	tablespoon dry yeast
1¹/2	cups warm (100 degrees) water
¹/4	cup olive oil
5¹/2	cups flour
4	teaspoons sea salt
4	tablespoons olive oil

Dissolve the yeast in the warm water in a ceramic bowl. Let stand for 10 minutes to proof. Stir in ¹/4 cup olive oil. Place the flour and 2 teaspoons of the sea salt in a mixing bowl. Add the yeast mixture. Beat at medium speed for 3 minutes. Place the dough in a lightly oiled large ceramic bowl, turning to coat the surface. Cover the bowl with plastic wrap. Let rise for 1 to 1¹/2 hours or until doubled in bulk.

Divide the dough into 2 equal portions. Flatten and stretch each portion to cover the bottom of an oiled 10×15-inch baking pan. Drizzle each with 1 tablespoon olive oil. Cover with plastic wrap. Let rest for 10 minutes. Uncover each pan and restretch the dough to cover the bottom of the pans completely. Cover each pan with a towel. Let rise for 25 minutes. Brush with the remaining 2 tablespoons olive oil. Sprinkle with the remaining 2 teaspoons sea salt. Place on the upper oven rack. Bake at 425 degrees for 20 to 25 minutes or until golden brown. Brush the top with additional olive oil if desired.

Makes two 10×15-inch loaves

V A R I A T I O N S

For *Rosemary Focaccia,* add 2 tablespoons chopped fresh rosemary to the dough during the beating process.

For *Black Olive Focaccia,* add ¹/2 cup slivered pitted kalamata olives to the dough at the end of the beating process. (Note: The dough will turn a dark color if you add the olives too early.)

For *Caramelized Red Onion and Gorgonzola Focaccia,* slice 1 red onion and sauté in 1 tablespoon vegetable oil in a skillet. After baking for 15 minutes, top focaccia with the sautéed onion and 6 ounces of Gorgonzola cheese. Return to the oven and bake for 12 to 15 minutes longer.

CHEESE BISCUITS

The real beauty of these Cheese Biscuits (besides the cheese) is that there's no rolling or cutting involved. You simply drop them onto the baking sheet. Make these when every other part of the meal is picked up from the deli, freezer case, or salad bar. People will think you fussed.

BISCUITS FOR DESSERT!

For warm **Apple Shortcake with Cinnamon Ice Cream,** prepare the Cheese Biscuits as directed (above right). Peel, core and slice 4 Golden Delicious apples. Sauté in 2 tablespoons unsalted butter in a skillet. Add 2 tablespoons sugar and 2 tablespoons brandy and cook until the apples are soft. Warm 1 cup of store-purchased applesauce. To serve, open each warm biscuit and place 1/4 cup applesauce and 1/4 of the sautéed apples on the bottom. Cover with the top of the biscuit and sprinkle with confectioners' sugar. Serve with a scoop of cinnamon ice cream.

From the Longaberger Pantry

CHEESE BISCUITS

2	cups flour
2 1/2	teaspoons baking powder
1	teaspoon salt
1/4	cup chilled shortening
1/2	cup shredded sharp Cheddar cheese
2/3	cup milk
1/4	cup (1/2 stick) butter, melted

Mix the flour, baking powder and salt in a bowl. Cut in the shortening and Cheddar cheese until crumbly. Add the milk and stir to incorporate. Drop by rounded spoonfuls onto an ungreased baking sheet. Bake at 450 degrees for 8 to 10 minutes or until golden brown. Brush with melted butter and serve immediately.

Makes 6 to 8 large biscuits, or 12 small biscuits

VARIATIONS

For *Spicy Cheese Biscuits,* add 2 tablespoons chopped chiles, 1/2 teaspoon cumin and 1/4 cup chopped fresh parsley or cilantro to the batter.

For *Plain Biscuits,* eliminate the Cheddar cheese and increase the shortening to 6 tablespoons and the milk to 1 cup. (Note: If you want your biscuits to have a more definite shape, bake in greased muffin cups.) These biscuits can be used to make sandwiches or strawberry shortcake not so plain.

SMART TIP

KEEP BISCUITS
TOASTY WARM

Just place one of our pottery Bricks in the oven and heat for 10 minutes, then place it, wrapped in a napkin, in a basket underneath your biscuits. Bricks come in several sizes and work equally well for serving breads, rolls, tortillas, muffins— whatever you need to keep warm . . . or cold! Bricks go in the freezer, too!

ROOM FOR DESSERT?

Grandma Bonnie Longaberger, our founder's mom, always served dessert after family dinners. Her twelve pie-loving children expected it! All of us here at Longaberger® are dessert lovers, too, and we've had a decadent time selecting, testing, and tasting this assortment of classic American desserts. If you're looking forward to a sweet treat from the oven, remember that baking is an exact science; you'll get better results if you measure accurately, and don't alter quantities or delete ingredients. And as with any recipe, your desserts will turn out exceptionally well if they're made with exceptional ingredients, so be sure to keep your pantry stocked with plenty of fresh eggs and cream, unsalted butter, quality chocolate, and the freshest fruits of the season.

ADDICTED TO CHOCOLATE?

Ancient Aztecs valued gold and cocoa beans equally, and those of us who love chocolate understand why. To us, if dessert doesn't include chocolate, really, what's the point? There's scientific evidence that says our insatiable appetite for chocolate may literally be all in our heads—chemicals found in chocolate are similar to those released in the brain when we're falling in love. Christopher Columbus was the first European to discover cocoa. Other explorers observed the importance the Indians placed on "cacao" beans, which were ground and mixed with water or wine to make a frothy beverage seasoned with vanilla, pimento, or chiles. Eventually chocolate made its way across the Atlantic, where few acquired the taste for it, save for those who drank it for its perceived medicinal qualities. Only when some bright thinker combined the bitter stuff with sugar did this early-day "hot chocolate" gain favor. Initially reserved for royalty and the very rich, chocolate spread to the masses as it became more widely obtainable, and therefore cheaper. Not until 1834 did a Dutch chocolate maker patent a method for making cocoa powder, which could be remixed with cocoa butter to create the solid chocolate bars we know and love today.

MORE FUN FACTS

Cacao trees only flourish in regions of the world located within 20 degrees north or south of the equator. Only 10 to 30 percent of each tree's blossoms will mature into cocoa pods. Each cocoa pod contains 20 to 50 beans. The beans are extracted from the pods, then fermented, which causes the beans to lose some of their bitterness and develop the essential oils that carry the chocolate flavor. The beans are then dried and processed into finished chocolate.

CHOCOLATE BASICS

Always bake with good-quality chocolate. In general, French, Belgian, and Swiss chocolates have a higher cocoa butter content, a richer flavor, and a smoother texture than American chocolates. Valrhona, Callebaut, and Schraffenburger are all excellent brands to use. If you only have chocolate chips in your pantry, adding an extra tablespoon of sweet unsalted butter will help.

Microwaving makes short work of melting chocolate. We prefer microwaving over the outmoded double-boiler method because there is no water or steam to make the chocolate "seize." When microwaving chocolate, chop it first into small pieces, and place it in the microwave for small increments of time. Take it out while there are still some soft lumps, stir, and then let the residual heat finish the job.

FLAVORS

Chocolate	Liquor	Sugar	Additives
Unsweetened	100%		
Bittersweet	35%	some	
Semisweet	35%	some	
Sweet	15%	some	some
Milk	10%	some	12% whole milk

THE GREAT AMERICAN BROWNIE

There are two camps of brownie bakers: Those who prefer a dense, fudge-like texture and those who crave a more cake-like brownie. If you're in the first camp, this recipe is for you. And here's an added surprise: The entire recipe is whipped up in a single saucepan!

THE GREAT AMERICAN BROWNIE		From the Longaberger Pantry
6	tablespoons unsalted butter	
4	ounces semisweet chocolate	
2	(1-ounce) squares unsweetened chocolate	
1/2	cup sugar	
1/2	cup packed brown sugar	
2	eggs	
1/2	cup unsifted flour	
1/4	teaspoon salt	
1/2	teaspoon vanilla extract	
	Confectioners' sugar	
	Dutch cocoa	
	Fresh strawberries	

Melt the butter, semisweet chocolate and unsweetened chocolate in a large heavy saucepan over low heat. Remove from the heat. Add the sugar, brown sugar, eggs, flour, salt and vanilla in the order listed, beating well after each addition. Pour into a greased foil-lined 8×8-inch baking dish. Bake at 350 degrees for 25 minutes or until the brownies just begin to pull from the sides of the dish. Cool in the dish on a wire rack to room temperature. Chill for several hours.

To serve, remove the brownies from the dish by inverting onto a cutting board. Remove the foil. Cut the brownies into 1×1-inch pieces. Place half the brownies on a plate and dust with confectioners' sugar. Place the remaining brownies on another plate and dust with Dutch cocoa. Arrange both sets of brownies in alternating concentric circles on a serving platter, placing fresh strawberries in the center. This presentation is perfect for a lunch meeting, the children's after-school snack or part of a dessert buffet.

Makes 16 large brownies

V A R I A T I O N S

For **Loaded Brownies,** (pictured above left) add either 1 cup Heath® toffee pieces, 1 cup chocolate chips, 1 cup mixed nuts, 1 cup crushed peanut butter cups or 1 to 1 1/2 cups of a mixture of each (for example, 1/2 cup peanuts and 1/2 cup peanut butter cups) to the batter.

RASPBERRY SAUCE

From the
Longaberger
Pantry

1	(10-ounce) package frozen raspberries
1/2	cup sugar
1	tablespoon fresh lemon juice

Combine the raspberries, sugar and lemon juice in a saucepan. Bring to a boil over low heat, stirring occasionally. Cook for 6 minutes or until of the desired consistency. (Note: You may microwave on High for 3 to 5 minutes, stirring at 1-minute intervals.) Press the sauce through a sieve into a bowl, discarding the seeds. Return to the saucepan. Cook over low heat until thickened, stirring constantly. Continue to cook until the mixture is reduced to 3/4 cup. Chill immediately, stirring frequently while cooling.

CHOCOLATE GANACHE

From the
Longaberger
Pantry

1/4	cup heavy cream
6	ounces bittersweet chocolate, chopped, or 10 ounces white chocolate, chopped

Bring the cream to a boil in a small heavy saucepan. Remove from the heat. Add the bittersweet chocolate or white chocolate. Cover with a lid or plastic wrap. Let stand for 3 minutes. Uncover and stir the ganache until smooth. Pour over brownies and spread to cover.

HOT FUDGE SAUCE

From the
Longaberger
Pantry

3	ounces unsweetened baking chocolate
2	tablespoons unsalted butter
10	tablespoons heavy cream
1/4	cup milk
1/2	cup corn syrup

Microwave the chocolate and butter in a microwave-safe dish on Low until melted, being careful not to burn the chocolate. Bring the cream, milk and corn syrup to a boil in a heavy saucepan. Boil for 1 minute, stirring constantly. Reduce the heat. Add the chocolate mixture and stir to mix well. Do not boil or the sauce will become grainy. Remove from the heat. Serve warm.

PECAN DIAMONDS

These are sumptuous cookies, with a rich, shortbread-cookie crust studded with glistening, gooey caramel pecans. Have tall glasses of cold milk ready.

PECAN DIAMONDS

From the Longaberger Pantry

1	cup (2 sticks) unsalted butter, softened
2/3	cup confectioners' sugar
1	egg
3	cups flour
2/3	cup unsalted butter
1/2	cup honey
3/4	cup packed brown sugar
1/4	cup sugar
3	tablespoons heavy cream
4	cups pecans, coarsely chopped

Line our 9×13-inch Baking Dish with foil and then butter the foil. Cream 1 cup butter and confectioners' sugar in a mixing bowl until light and fluffy. Beat in the egg. Add the flour all at once. Beat at low speed until the dough is smooth and holds together. Press the dough into the prepared pan. Prick all over with a fork. Chill for 15 to 20 minutes. Bake at 375 degrees for 20 minutes or until slightly golden brown.

Melt 2/3 cup butter with the honey in a heavy saucepan. Add the brown sugar and sugar. Bring to a boil. Boil for 1 minute. Remove from the heat. Add the cream and pecans. Mix until all of the pecans are coated. Pour onto the baked crust. Bake for 20 to 25 minutes. Cool completely. Lift from the dish using the foil edges and place on a cutting board. Cut into diamond shapes to the desired size. Store in an airtight container.

Makes 36 to 50 cookies

V A R I A T I O N

For *Mixed Nut Diamonds with Chocolate Drizzle,* substitute a mixture of macadamia nuts, hazelnuts and cashews for the pecans. Cool bars and then drizzle warm Bittersweet Chocolate Ganache (page 149) over the top. Let stand until set before cutting into diamonds.

YUM-YUM SQUARES

The recipe for these bar cookies comes from a school cafeteria in nearby Cuyahoga Falls, Ohio. They're double-layered, no-bake, after-school yummy treats that simply melt in your mouth. Our families have loved them for years. Bet yours will too.

YUM-YUM SQUARES		From the Longaberger Pantry
2	cups peanut butter	1/2	cup packed
2 1/2	cups confectioners' sugar		brown sugar
		1/2	teaspoon vanilla extract
1	cup graham cracker crumbs (about 6 graham crackers)	2	cups semisweet or white chocolate chips
1/2	cup (1 stick) unsalted butter, melted	1	tablespoon shortening

Combine the peanut butter, confectioners' sugar, graham cracker crumbs, butter, brown sugar and vanilla in a large bowl and mix well. Press into a 10×15-inch baking pan. Melt the chocolate chips and shortening in a small saucepan. Spread over the peanut butter layer to cover. Chill in the refrigerator until firm. Cut into squares.
Makes 4 dozen

LEMON DROPS

These wonderful shortbread cookies have a light and tangy icing and are just the thing with a spot of hot tea. Make the kids happy and toss some colored sprinkles across the icing before it sets. Or, if you've got fresh nuts in the pantry, stir some—chopped—in after the flour and salt.

LEMON DROPS		From the Longaberger Pantry
1/2	cup unsweetened butter, softened	1 1/2	teaspoons chopped lemon zest
1/2	cup confectioners' sugar	1 1/4	cups flour
		1/2	teaspoon salt
1/2	teaspoon vanilla extract		Lemon Glaze (facing page)

Cream the butter and confectioners' sugar in a mixing bowl until light and fluffy. Add the vanilla and lemon zest. Mix in the flour and salt until smooth. Chill for 1 to 2 hours.

Roll the dough gently 1/2 inch thick on a lightly floured surface. Cut into small circles using a round cookie cutter. Place on a cookie sheet lined with baking parchment or foil. Press a small indentation in the center of each circle. Bake at 375 degrees for 15 to 20 minutes or until light golden brown around the edges. Cool on a wire rack. Place a small dollop of Lemon Glaze on top of each cookie.
Makes 24 to 30 small cookies

LEMON GLAZE

From the
Longaberger
Pantry

1/4	cup (1/2 stick) unsweetened butter, melted
1/4	cup strained fresh lemon juice
1	(1-pound) package confectioners' sugar
1	drop of yellow food coloring

Combine the butter, lemon juice, confectioners' sugar and food coloring in a mixing bowl and beat until smooth.

ORANGE ALMOND BISCOTTI

The word biscotti means "cooked again," and indeed these are baked twice. Distinctively hard and crunchy, they're especially fine for dunking in coffee and keep practically forever in the cookie jar on the counter. Better double the recipe because they disappear fast.

ORANGE ALMOND BISCOTTI	From the Longaberger Pantry
1	cup slivered almonds, lightly toasted
1	cup sugar
1/2	cup (1 stick) unsalted butter, melted
2	tablespoons orange juice
2	tablespoons grated orange zest
3	eggs
1	teaspoon vanilla extract
3	cups flour
2	teaspoons baking powder
1/2	teaspoon salt
1	egg, beaten
	Coarse sugar for sprinkling

Chop the almonds coarsely in a food processor. Combine the almonds, sugar, butter, orange juice, orange zest, 3 eggs and vanilla in a mixing bowl and mix well. Stir in the flour, baking powder and salt. Knead briefly on a lightly floured surface until the dough is no longer sticky, adding additional flour if needed. Shape into a long loaf about 2 inches wide. Place on a parchment-lined or greased cookie sheet. Brush with the beaten egg and sprinkle with coarse sugar. Bake at 350 degrees on the middle oven rack for 25 minutes or until firm to the touch. Remove from the oven and let cool slightly. The loaf will have a cake-like texture. Reduce the oven temperature to 300 degrees. Cut the loaf diagonally into 1-inch slices. Place on a cookie sheet. Bake for 20 minutes or until slightly soft in the center. Remove from the cookie sheet to a wire rack to cool. The cookies will harden as they cool. Store in airtight containers.

Makes 26 cookies

VARIATIONS

For **Pistachio Lemon Cranberry Biscotti,** substitute pistachios for the almonds and lemon juice and zest for the orange juice and zest. Add 1 cup plumped dried cranberries.

For **Mocha Biscotti,** omit the orange juice and zest. Add 2 tablespoons strong brewed coffee, 1 tablespoon finely ground coffee beans and 1/2 cup chopped bittersweet chocolate.

CLASSIC CHEESECAKE

Cheesecakes are tremendously popular, and it's no wonder. They're intensely satisfying. The options for variations are endless. And they can be made ahead of time and kept in the refrigerator for up to two days before serving or stored in the freezer for up to a month. (Thaw cheesecakes in the refrigerator for twenty-four hours before serving.)

CLASSIC CHEESECAKE			From the Longaberger Pantry
2	cups graham cracker crumbs	3/4	cup sugar
		3	eggs
2	tablespoons sugar	1	tablespoon fresh
1/4	cup (1/2 stick)		lemon juice
	unsalted butter or	1	teaspoon vanilla
	margarine, melted		extract
24	ounces cream	1	cup sour cream
	cheese, softened	3	tablespoons sugar

Combine the graham cracker crumbs, 2 tablespoons sugar and butter in a bowl and mix well. Press evenly over the bottom and up the side of a 9-inch springform pan. Bake at 350 degrees for 5 to 6 minutes or until brown. Let stand until cool. Beat the cream cheese in a mixing bowl until light and fluffy. Add 3/4 cup sugar gradually, beating until smooth. Beat in the eggs 1 at a time. Stir in the lemon juice and vanilla. Spoon into the prepared pan. Bake at 375 degrees for 40 to 45 minutes or until set. Increase the oven temperature to 450 degrees. Mix the sour cream and 3 tablespoons sugar in a bowl. Spread evenly over the hot cheesecake. Bake for 5 minutes. Cool on a wire rack to room temperature. Chill, covered, for 8 hours or longer. Remove the side of the pan. Garnish with fresh fruit, such as raspberries and peaches.

Serves 12

V A R I A T I O N S

For *Pumpkin Cheesecake,* prepare Walnut Gingersnap Crust (facing page). Add 2 cups canned pumpkin purée and 1 teaspoon each ground ginger, cinnamon and nutmeg to the filling above. Use the sour cream topping. Bake for 45 minutes.

For *Chocolate Almond Cheesecake,* prepare Amaretti Cookie Crust (facing page). Omit the lemon juice and add 5 ounces melted bittersweet chocolate, 1 teaspoon almond extract and 4 ounces almond paste to the filling above. (Cream the almond paste first and then add the cream cheese.) The sour cream topping is optional. Bake for 45 minutes.

For *Chocolate Brownie Cheesecake,* prepare Chocolate Crumb Crust (facing page). Omit the lemon juice and fold 2 cups frozen 1-inch brownie pieces into the filling above. Omit the sour cream topping. Bake for 40 minutes.

Crusts

The crust of the cheesecake can be a simple way to make a variation without much effort. The following is a list of variations from the crust recipe on the previous page.

For *Walnut Gingersnap Crust*, combine 3¹/₂ ounces walnuts, chopped, ¹/₂ cup (1 stick) unsalted butter, melted, 2 tablespoons sugar and 1¹/₄ cups fine gingersnap crumbs in a bowl and mix well. Press over the bottom of a 9-inch springform pan. Bake at 375 degrees for 10 minutes.

For *Amaretti Cookie Crust,* combine 1 cup amaretti cookie crumbs, 1 cup graham cracker crumbs, 2 tablespoons sugar and ¹/₂ cup (1 stick) unsalted butter, melted, in a bowl and mix well. Press over the bottom of a 9-inch springform pan. Bake at 350 degrees for 7 to 10 minutes.

For *Chocolate Crumb Crust,* process 1 package chocolate wafers in a blender to make very fine crumbs (about 2 cups). Mix the crumbs, 2 tablespoons sugar and 7 tablespoons unsalted butter, melted, in a bowl. Press firmly over the bottom of a 9-inch springform pan. Bake at 350 degrees for 7 to 10 minutes.

TAMI'S FAVORITE GINGERBREAD

Did you know that the recipe for gingerbread is seven centuries old? Originally, gingerbread was a baked mixture of cake and bread crumbs, honey and spices. This version is spicy, cake-like, and addictive. It's lovely by itself or embellished with a sauté of pears and figs, drizzled with a caramel sauce, or christened with a dollop of Lemon Curd (below right).

SMART TIP
REMEMBER MOLASSES?

It's a pity you don't find molasses in too many pantries anymore, because the dark, sticky syrup contains more iron and calcium than other sweeteners. Good in soft molasses cookies, great mixed with equal parts balsamic vinegar and brushed onto grilled meats, molasses also comes in handy when you run out of brown sugar. Just mix 1/4 cup molasses with 1 cup sugar to replace light brown sugar; mix 1/2 cup molasses with 1 cup sugar to replace dark brown sugar. And try this neat trick: Rinse your measuring cup with water before measuring molasses or other sticky sweeteners. They'll slide right out.

TAMI'S FAVORITE GINGERBREAD			From the Longaberger Pantry
1/2	cup (1 stick) butter, softened	1/2	teaspoon salt
1	cup sugar	11/2	teaspoons ground ginger
2	large eggs	3/4	cup molasses
21/2	cups flour	1	cup hot water
11/2	teaspoons baking soda		

Beat the butter in a mixing bowl until smooth. Add the sugar and beat until light and fluffy. Beat in the eggs. Add the flour, baking soda, salt and ginger and mix well. Stir in the molasses and hot water. Pour into a buttered and lightly floured 9×9-inch cake pan. Bake at 350 degrees for 35 to 40 minutes or until a wooden pick inserted into the center comes out clean. Cut into squares.

Makes 9 squares

VARIATION

For *Crumble Topped Gingerbread* (pictured), mix 2 tablespoons flour with 1 tablespoon sugar. Cut in 1 tablespoon butter until crumbly. Sprinkle on top before baking as directed above. Serve with Lemon Curd (below).

LEMON CURD		From the Longaberger Pantry
3	eggs	
1/2	cup fresh lemon juice	
1	cup sugar	
1/2	cup (1 stick) unsalted butter, melted	

Beat the eggs in a double boiler until frothy. Stir in the lemon juice, sugar and butter. Cook over simmering water for 16 minutes or until slightly thickened, stirring constantly. Remove from the heat. Spoon into a small container. Let cool to room temperature. Chill, covered, for at least 2 hours before serving.

Makes 13/4 cups

ALMOND CAKE WITH RASPBERRY SAUCE

This cake's rich almond flavor comes from almond paste—look for it in your grocery store's baking aisle. Here, we've completely covered the cake with fruits to give it a glorious jewel-encrusted look. Short on time? Tumble a half pint of fresh, whole raspberries on top. Don't count on leftovers.

ALMOND CAKE	From the Longaberger Pantry
1/2 cup (1 stick) unsalted butter, softened	
3/4 cup sugar	
8 ounces almond paste	
3 eggs	
1 tablespoon Triple Sec	
1 teaspoon almond extract	
1/4 cup flour	
1/3 teaspoon baking powder	
Confectioners' sugar	
Raspberry Sauce (page 149)	

Line a 9-inch round cake pan with waxed paper. Butter and flour the waxed paper. Cream the butter, sugar and almond paste in a mixing bowl until light and fluffy. Add the eggs, liqueur and almond extract and mix well. Add the flour and baking powder and mix just until blended. Pour into the prepared pan. Bake at 350 degrees for 40 to 45 minutes or until a wooden pick inserted into the center comes out clean. Cool in the pan. Invert onto a serving plate. Sprinkle with confectioners' sugar. Serve Raspberry Sauce over or under the cake. (Note: You may use 1/4 teaspoon orange extract and 1 teaspoon vanilla extract instead of the Triple Sec.)

Serves 8

SERVING TIP
LACY CAKES

For a quick and impressive cake decoration, place a clean paper doily over an unfrosted cake top, and sprinkle confectioners' sugar over the doily. Peel away the doily very carefully to reveal the intricate pattern left behind.

GOLDEN POUND CAKES

We hear that patrons of New York coffeehouses really go for thick slices of this luxe pound cake, accompanied by a big cup of gourmet coffee. Six slices tucked inside a plastic food storage bag sell fast at bake sales. Throw together several of these golden loaves at once, then stash them in the freezer for impromptu guests.

GOLDEN POUND CAKES	From the Longaberger Pantry
2 cups flour	
1 (1-pound) package confectioners' sugar	
Pinch of salt	
1 1/2 cups (3 sticks) unsalted butter, softened	
6 eggs	
1 teaspoon almond extract	
1 teaspoon vanilla extract	

Mix the flour, confectioners' sugar and salt in a mixing bowl. Cut in the butter until the mixture is crumbly and resembles coarse cornmeal. Mix the eggs and almond and vanilla extracts in a small bowl. Add to the flour mixture. Beat at medium speed for 2 minutes. Pour into 2 greased and floured 5×9-inch loaf pans. Bake at 350 degrees for 50 to 55 minutes or until a wooden pick inserted into the center of each loaf tests done, covering with foil during the last 10 minutes to prevent over browning. Cool in the pans for a few minutes. Invert onto wire racks to cool completely.

Makes 2 loaves

VARIATIONS

An easy way to change the look of this cake is by varying the cake pan you use. Try using a tube pan, decorated bundt pan, small loaf pans, muffin pans or our Small Pottery Crocks.

For *Citrus Poppy Seed Pound Cakes,* add 3 tablespoons poppy seeds, 2 tablespoons lemon juice, 1 tablespoon grated lemon zest and 1 tablespoon grated orange zest. Prepare a *Lemon Glaze* by bringing 1/2 cup sugar, 1/3 cup fresh lemon juice and 1/3 cup water to a boil in a saucepan. Brush over the warm cakes.

For *Marbled Pound Cake,* reserve 1/3 of the batter and stir in 2 ounces bittersweet chocolate. Layer 1/2 of the remaining batter, the chocolate batter and the remaining batter in the prepared pan. Swirl to marbleize. Bake as above.

For *Rum Pound Cakes,* add 2 teaspoons rum extract to the recipe above. Prepare a *Rum Glaze* by melting 2 tablespoons unsalted butter in a saucepan. Add 1/4 cup sugar and 1/4 cup dark rum and bring to a boil. Brush over the warm cakes.

APPLE ORCHARD CAKE

Fresh chopped apples make this cake exceptionally moist and chunky. Topped with sautéed apples and whipped cream, it makes a fine dessert. We've also been known to whip one of these up on a Sunday morning to enjoy with coffee and the morning paper.

APPLE ORCHARD CAKE

From the
Longaberger
Pantry

4	eggs
1	cup vegetable oil
2	cups sugar
2	teaspoons vanilla extract
3	cups chopped Golden Delicious apples
3	cups sifted flour
1/2	teaspoon cinnamon
1	teaspoon baking soda
1	cup chopped pecans

Beat the eggs in a large mixing bowl. Add the oil, sugar and vanilla and mix well. Stir in the apples. Add the flour, cinnamon and baking soda and stir gently. Add the pecans and mix well. Pour into a greased and floured 9×13-inch cake pan. (Our 9×13-inch Baking Dish works well too.) Bake at 325 degrees for 1 hour or until a wooden pick inserted into the center of the cake comes out clean.

Serves 12

SERVING TIP

IN PURSUIT OF PERFECT WHIPPED CREAM

Start with cream that is at least 30% butterfat—"heavy" cream is usually around 36% butterfat. Today's cream is ultra-pasteurized to give it a longer shelf life; sadly, this process also lessens the ability of the cream to incorporate air and become light and fluffy. The cream, bowl, and whisk should be cold. Whip the cream by hand or use a mixer. If you use a mixer, finish whipping by hand with a wire whisk to reduce the chance of turning the cream to butter (softer peaks look better anyway). Add sugar and vanilla extract to the cream late in the process. Adding it earlier decreases volume. Cover whipped cream so that the plastic wrap comes into contact with the entire surface of the cream. (Cream picks up odors easily.) Refrigerate until ready to use.

CHOCOLATE PUDDING PIE

Like the chocolate pies found in rotating glass cases in neighborhood diners, this one has a deep chocolate cream filling paired with a frothy, mile-high whipped meringue. Use high-quality chocolate for this—you'll taste the difference. Present this beauty sliced, atop dessert plates lightly dusted with baking cocoa.

PREPARATION TIP
CONQUERING MERINGUE

There's no doubt that meringue can be temperamental. Failure isn't due to humid weather, as is widely believed, but to overcooking or undercooking. When making a meringue-topped pie, make the filling first, then keep it warm while you complete the meringue. Always put meringue on warm filling. A dusting of fine cake crumbs between the hot filling and meringue will keep the filling from "weeping." The filling will also weep if the sugar is not dissolved properly in the beaten egg whites, so gradually add sugar to the egg whites, about a tablespoon at a time. Many find that adding 1/4 teaspoon cream of tartar will add stability to meringues.

CHOCOLATE PUDDING PIE	From the Longaberger Pantry
1/2	cup (1 stick) unsalted butter
3	ounces bittersweet chocolate
1	cup sugar
3	tablespoons cornstarch
3	tablespoons baking cocoa
1	(12-ounce) can evaporated milk
1/2	cup (about) milk
3	egg yolks, beaten
1	teaspoon vanilla extract
1	baked (9-inch) pie shell
	Foolproof Meringue (below)

Melt the butter and chocolate in a heavy saucepan. Mix the sugar, cornstarch and baking cocoa in a small bowl. Add to the melted butter and blend well. Pour the evaporated milk into a 2-cup measure. Add enough milk to measure 2 cups. Stir into the chocolate mixture. Stir a small amount of the mixture into the beaten egg yolks; stir the egg yolks into the mixture. Add the vanilla. Cook until thickened, stirring constantly. Pour into the pie shell. Spread Foolproof Meringue over the filling, sealing to the edge. Bake at 450 degrees for 5 to 7 minutes or until golden brown. Chill, covered, in the refrigerator.

Serves 8

FOOLPROOF MERINGUE			From the Longaberger Pantry
6	tablespoons sugar	1/2	teaspoon vanilla
1	tablespoon		extract
	cornstarch	3	egg whites
1/2	cup water		Salt to taste

Combine the sugar, cornstarch and water in a small saucepan. Cook for 5 minutes or until clear and thickened, stirring constantly. Cool slightly. Add the vanilla. Beat the egg whites and salt in a mixing bowl until soft peaks form. Add the syrup gradually, beating constantly until stiff peaks form.

GRANDMA BONNIE'S APPLE PIE

Grandma Bonnie Longaberger is the matriarch of the Longaberger clan. The mother of twelve children, she insisted on treating her family to dessert every night. When dessert was pie, as it was most often, she'd bake up three or four at once and cut each into four huge servings. Always efficient, she simply saved her family the trouble of asking for seconds of pie! We think any pie tastes best made in the extra-deep, wide-rimmed pie plate we named for her (pictured on the facing page).

SMART TIP

WHICH APPLE GOES WHERE?

The chart on the facing page is a guide to matching the right apple to the right dessert. The best pies are filled with a combination of apple varieties. Mix a few soft apples with firmer apples, and your pie will hold its shape better during baking. The filling will have a more complex flavor, too.

GRANDMA BONNIE'S APPLE PIE		From the Longaberger Pantry
3	cups sliced peeled apples	
1	cup sugar	
3	tablespoons flour	
1/2	teaspoon cinnamon	
	Pie Pastry (below)	
2	tablespoons unsalted butter or margarine, cut into pieces	
3	tablespoons milk	

Mix the apples, sugar, flour and cinnamon in a large bowl. Divide the Pie Pastry into 2 equal portions. Roll each portion into a 12-inch circle on a lightly floured surface. Fit 1 pastry circle into a 9-inch deep-dish pie plate, trimming and fluting the edge. Prick the bottom with a fork. Add the apple filling. Dot with the butter and sprinkle with the milk. Cut the remaining pastry circle into strips. Weave lattice-fashion over the pie. Or place the whole remaining pastry circle on top of the filling, sealing and fluting the edge and cutting vents. Bake at 375 degrees for 40 to 45 minutes or until golden brown.

Serves 4 to 8

PIE PASTRY				From the Longaberger Pantry
2	cups flour	1	small egg, beaten	
1/2	tablespoon sugar	1/4	cup water	
3/4	teaspoon salt	1/2	tablespoon vinegar	
3/4	cup lard			

Sift the flour, sugar and salt in a bowl. Cut in the lard until the mixture resembles coarse crumbs. Mix the egg, water and vinegar in a bowl. Add to the flour mixture and mix until the dough is moist enough to form a soft ball. Wrap in plastic wrap. Chill for 30 minutes.

Makes enough pastry for a double-crust pie

A Handy Apple Reference Chart

Cortland, October–January, Mildly sweet and tender texture. Soft and loses its shape when baked.

Empire, September–January, Balanced with sweet and tartness. Juicy apple, soft, loses its shape when baked.

Golden Delicious, September–May, Mild flavor profile. Soft and mushy when baked. Holds its shape when baked.

Granny Smith, September–July, Tart and holds it shape when baked. Works best when paired with another apple.

Jonathan, September–January, Tart, tender, and crisp texture. Loses shape when baked.

McIntosh, September–June, Slightly tart, juicy when baked, and very soft when baked, similar to applesauce.

Rome Beauty, October–June, Perfumey and sweet. Holds its shape when baked but has a soft bite.

Winesap, October–June, Sweet and spicy flavor, firm texture, and holds its shape when baked.

FRESH APRICOT DEEP-DISH PIE

A spunky, fresh-tasting pie that also works well with fresh nectarines. Try making it with frozen peaches in the dead of winter, when you begin to doubt that summer really does exist.

OH, NO!
PIE FILLING
OVERBOARD!

To keep your pie filling from overflowing onto the bottom of your oven, place your pie on a jelly roll pan lined with foil before baking.

FRESH APRICOT DEEP-DISH PIE		From the Longaberger Pantry
3 1/2	cups peeled apricot halves	1/4 cup slivered almonds, toasted (optional)
1/4	cup water	Grandma Bonnie's
1 1/2	cups sugar	Pie Pastry (page 168)
1/2	teaspoon nutmeg	
1/4	teaspoon salt	1 egg
2	tablespoons unsalted butter or margarine	1 tablespoon water

Combine the apricot halves and 1/4 cup water in a saucepan. Bring to a boil. Stir in the sugar, nutmeg and salt. Spoon into a buttered 1- to 1 1/2-quart round baking dish. Dot with the butter. Sprinkle with the almonds.

Shape the Pie Pastry into a ball on a lightly floured surface. Flatten the ball to a thickness of 1/2 inch. Roll into an 11-inch circle. Roll the pastry carefully around a rolling pin and unroll over the pie filling. Fold the edge under and flute. Cut vents in the top. Brush with a mixture of the egg and 1 tablespoon water. Bake at 400 degrees for 15 minutes. Reduce the oven temperature to 350 degrees. Bake for 30 minutes longer or until golden brown.

Serves 8

Grandma Bonnie's Pie Pastry Advice

- "I like lard for piecrusts, but I don't use it anymore for health reasons. Whatever shortening you use—butter, lard or shortening—chill it well. That's the secret to a flaky crust."
- "I cut my shortening into 1-inch pieces before cutting it into my flour."
- "Make sure the water that's sprinkled over the flour is ice-cold. And be careful not to add too much water—you want just enough to hold the dough together."
- "After the dough is mixed, gather it into a ball and press it into a disk. Wrap it in waxed paper or plastic wrap, and put it in the fridge for at least 30 minutes. If it's very cold when you take it out again, let it rest a few minutes at room temperature."
- "Too much handling makes a tough crust."
- "You'll save time in the long run if you make up piecrust in big batches, then divide it up into the amount you'll use at any one time. It'll keep in the freezer for up to 2 months."

APPLE RAISIN FRENCH BREAD PUDDING WITH RUM SAUCE

Bread pudding reminds us of rocking chairs and hand-knit afghans because it never goes out of style and it makes you feel good all over. Fresh apples and plump raisins make this one extra special.

SMART TIP

THERE'S NO EXCUSE FOR NOT MAKING BREAD PUDDING

Best warm from the oven, leftover bread pudding isn't bad eaten cold right out of the pan for breakfast either. Bread pudding can be assembled ahead of time and chilled in the refrigerator for 2 to 12 hours before baking. Just be sure to remove it from the refrigerator 2 hours before baking. Individual servings of bread pudding look adorable in our Pottery Salt™ Crocks (facing page) or our Stackable Custard Cups. Bread pudding is also an excellent way to use up dry cinnamon-raisin bread or croissants.

APPLE RAISIN FRENCH BREAD PUDDING — From the Longaberger Pantry

1	(16-ounce) loaf dry French bread, torn into bite-size pieces
1	to 1 1/2 cups chopped peeled baking apples, such as Rome Beauty or Golden Delicious
1	cup raisins
4	eggs, beaten
4	cups milk
2	cups sugar
1	tablespoon vanilla extract
	Rum Sauce (below)

Combine the bread, apples and raisins in a large mixing bowl and toss to mix. Beat the eggs, milk, sugar and vanilla in a mixing bowl. Pour over the bread mixture. Let stand for 15 to 20 minutes or until the mixture is absorbed, stirring occasionally. Spoon into a greased 8×12-inch baking dish. Bake at 350 degrees for 35 minutes or until a knife inserted in the center comes out clean. Serve warm with Rum Sauce or vanilla ice cream.

Serves 8

RUM SAUCE — From the Longaberger Pantry

2	eggs
1/4	cup rum
1	cup confectioners' sugar
1	cup whipping cream, whipped

Beat the eggs in a saucepan. Add the rum and confectioners' sugar and mix well. Cook over low heat for 5 minutes or until thickened, stirring constantly. Remove from the heat. Fold into the whipped cream. (Note: You may substitute 2 teaspoons rum extract for the rum.)

Makes 2 cups

MAGIC LEMON PUDDING

What's magic about this dessert, besides the heavenly lemon flavor? It's the way the pudding separates while it bakes—one creamy custard layer on the bottom, another spongy and airy layer on top. Yum.

SMART TIP

THE LOWDOWN ON LEMONS

When buying lemons, look for smooth, bright-colored skins. Lemons should be firm and plump. Store them in a plastic bag in the refrigerator. Always use fresh, not bottled, lemon juice for cooking. To extract the most juice from a lemon, first either roll it firmly on the counter with the palm of your hand or pop it into the microwave for 10 seconds.

A squeeze of fresh lemon juice can dramatically lift otherwise dull, flat flavors.

A few drops jazz up winter tomatoes, canned tomato soups, or sizzling steaks hot off the grill. To keep fresh fruit from quickly turning brown, rub cut surfaces with lemon juice. Big sale on lemons? Stock up, squeeze them, and freeze the juice in ice cube trays. Bag the cubes once they freeze.

MAGIC LEMON PUDDING	From the Longaberger Pantry
3	tablespoons unsalted butter, softened
1/3	cup sugar
1/8	teaspoon salt
3	large egg yolks
3	tablespoons flour
1/4	cup strained fresh lemon juice
2	to 3 teaspoons grated lemon zest
1	cup milk
4	large egg whites, at room temperature
1/8	teaspoon salt
	Confectioners' sugar

Mix the butter, sugar and 1/8 teaspoon salt in a bowl until crumbly. Add the egg yolks and mix well. Stir in the flour until smooth. Add the lemon juice and lemon zest gradually, stirring constantly. Stir in the milk gradually. Beat the egg whites at medium speed in a mixing bowl for 1 minute or until frothy. Add 1/8 teaspoon salt. Beat at medium-high speed until the egg whites are stiff but still moist. Whisk 1/3 of the egg whites into the batter gently to loosen the mixture. Fold in the remaining egg whites. Spoon or ladle into buttered custard cups until full. Place the cups in an ovenproof baking dish. Pour water into the baking dish to come halfway up the side of the cups. Bake at 325 degrees for 30 minutes or until a knife inserted in the centers come out nearly clean. Let stand for 10 minutes in the water bath. Remove from the water and dust liberally with confectioners' sugar. Serve warm, at room temperature or chilled.

Serves 6

BLUEBERRY CRISP

We know a thing or two about fruit desserts because we're surrounded by orchards here in Ohio. In fact, the patriarch of the Longaberger family, J. W. Longaberger, created one of our most distinctive and popular baskets, the Fruit Basket, especially for area fruit growers. We like fruit crisps like this one because they can be assembled quickly from whatever fruits are fresh, plentiful, and on hand. Serve your crisps warm, topped with a scoop of vanilla ice cream or a generous dollop of fresh whipped cream.

PREPARATION TIP
CRISP FOR A CROWD?

Simply double the above ingredients. Use our 9×13-inch Baking Dish and increase the baking time by 10 to 15 minutes.

BLUEBERRY CRISP	From the Longaberger Pantry
4	cups blueberries
2	tablespoons water
3/4	cup flour
1	cup sugar or packed brown sugar
1	teaspoon cinnamon
1/4	teaspoon salt
1/2	cup (1 stick) unsalted butter, softened

Place the blueberries and water in a buttered 8- or 9-inch deep baking dish. Mix the flour, sugar, cinnamon and salt in a bowl. Cut in the butter until crumbly. Spread over the blueberries. Bake at 350 degrees for 35 minutes or until the top is golden brown. Serve with whipped cream or ice cream.

Serves 6 to 8

SEASONAL VARIATIONS

Different fruits are at their peak at different times of the year. So before planning dessert, stroll through the farmer's market first. What's gorgeous? There's your crisp. If you're feeling really adventurous, make up a combo fruit crisp. Here are a few tried-and-true combinations you may want to consider:

Spring—Try **Rhubarb and Strawberry Crisp.** Use 2 cups sliced strawberries and 2 cups sliced rhubarb instead of the blueberries. Omit the water and cinnamon and add 1/4 cup grated orange zest and 1/2 teaspoon nutmeg.

Summer—Try **Peach and Blueberry Crisp.** Substitute 2 cups sliced peaches for 2 cups of the blueberries.

Fall and Winter—Try **Apple Blackberry Pear Crisp.** Use 1 cup sliced apples, 2 cups blackberries and 1 cup sliced pears instead of the blueberries. Use a few tablespoons of chopped crystallized ginger instead of the cinnamon.

Sliced Summer Melon in Lime Syrup

This is a very pretty, colorful, and refreshing way to end a big meal. You can make the syrup in advance and keep it in the refrigerator for several weeks. If you're feeling flamboyant, serve the melon alongside sorbet, ice cream, or our Golden Pound Cakes on page 162.

SMART TIP
MORE ABOUT MELONS

There are two kinds of melons: watermelons and muskmelons. Muskmelons include cantaloupes, casabas, Crenshaws, honeydews, and Persians. When choosing a melon, your most important tool is your nose. Ripe melons have a fresh, fruity scent, however faint. Look for melons that are heavy for their size, without soft spots or mold.

SLICED SUMMER MELON IN LIME SYRUP	From the Longaberger Pantry
2/3	cup sugar
1/3	cup fresh lime juice
1/3	cup water
	Zest of 2 limes, removed in strips with a vegetable peeler
1/2	teaspoon ground cardamom, or to taste
8	cups (3/4- to 1-inch) honeydew melon balls or squares (2 (5-pound) melons)
10	to 12 julienne strips of lime peel
	Mint leaves

Simmer the sugar, lime juice, water, lime zest strips and cardamom in a small saucepan for 1 minute or until the sugar is dissolved, stirring constantly. Remove from the heat. Let stand until cool. Strain the syrup, discarding the lime zest. To serve, combine the melon balls and syrup in a medium bowl. Spoon into 6 glasses. Garnish with julienned strips of lime peel and mint leaves or serve with a generous dollop of whipped cream or yogurt.

Serves 6

PECAN PEACH SUNDAES

Sleek and sophisticated, this dessert is worth the effort. Forget bowls—serve these sunshine-hued sundaes in your favorite stemware.

SERVING TIP

SUPER SUNDAES

Instead of peaches and vanilla ice cream, try sliced bananas and coconut ice cream showered in chocolate shavings. Pure heaven. During the fall and winter months, try sliced apples over cinnamon ice cream.

PECAN PEACH SUNDAES			From the Longaberger Pantry
1	tablespoon fresh lemon juice	3	tablespoons heavy cream
3	large firm ripe peaches, peeled, thinly sliced	1/2	cup toasted pecans
6	tablespoons unsalted butter	1	tablespoon bourbon (optional)
1/2	cup packed brown sugar	2	cups Vanilla Bean Ice Cream (below)

Place the lemon juice in a medium bowl. Add the peaches and toss to coat well. Melt the butter in a heavy saucepan over medium heat. Add the brown sugar. Cook until thickened and bubbly, stirring constantly. Stir in the cream 1 tablespoon at a time. Cook for 3 minutes or until the brown sugar is dissolved and the sauce is thickened and smooth, stirring constantly. Stir in the peaches, pecans and bourbon. Cook for 1 minute or until the sauce is heated through, stirring constantly.

To serve, alternate layers of the peach sauce and ice cream in dessert bowls.
Serves 4

VANILLA BEAN ICE CREAM

The ice cream is ridiculously rich and custard-based, flecked with mahogany specks of real vanilla bean. You'll need an electric or hand-cranked ice cream maker for this one.

VANILLA BEAN ICE CREAM			From the Longaberger Pantry
1	cup milk	1	cup sugar
1/2	cup heavy cream	3	cups half-and-half
1	vanilla bean, split	2	teaspoons vanilla extract
3	eggs		

Simmer the milk, cream and vanilla bean halves in a saucepan. Remove from the heat and keep covered for 15 minutes. Beat the eggs and sugar in a mixing bowl until thick and pale yellow. Combine with the vanilla mixture. Cook over medium heat to 185 degrees on a candy thermometer. (The mixture should coat the back of a spoon.) Do not let the custard reach the boiling point. Pour the custard through a sieve into an ice cream freezer container. Stir in the half-and-half and vanilla. Freeze using the manufacturer's directions for your ice cream maker.

Makes 5 cups

BERRY GRANITA

What is granita? The root of the word, "grana," means "grain," which describes the texture of this icy dessert perfectly. A cousin of sorts to sorbet, granita is essentially sweetened fruit juices captured in ice crystals. Get the kids to help out with this dessert—it's fun to make.

BERRY GRANITA	From the Longaberger Pantry
2 pints strawberries	
2 pints blueberries	
2 pints raspberries	
2 cups honey	
1 cup water	

Bring the strawberries, blueberries, raspberries, honey and water to a boil in a heavy saucepan. Purée in a blender or use a hand mixer. Pour through a strainer into a flat rectangular plastic container with a tight-fitting lid. Freeze, covered, for 2 hours or until slushy, stirring occasionally. Freeze for 10 hours longer or until firm, stirring once or twice. Scoop into chilled bowls to serve.

Serves 10 to 12

ACKNOWLEDGEMENTS

We hope that you will enjoy *Fresh from the Pantry* as much as we enjoyed creating it. This book would not have been possible without the dedication and support of many Longaberger® employees. We would also like to thank the following contributors for their time, ideas, and expertise.

Food Consultant and Stylist:	Sharon Reiss
Creative Consultant:	Keith Keegan
Writer:	Mary Douglas
Illustrations:	Nora Corbett
Food Photography:	Paul Poplis
Food Stylists:	Julie Garber, Mary Leber
Cover and Location Photography:	Colin McGuire
Prop Stylist:	Nora Corbett
Contributors:	Reid Boates, Steve Singular

A special thanks to Sharon Reiss and our own Sales Field Management who contributed recipes and creative ideas for this book. We hope we have captured the enthusiasm and interest they demonstrated for this project.

PROTECTOR GUIDE

Protectors serve two valuable functions—they protect your basket and they expand your basket's use. A variety of divided protectors is available. Use the chart below to help create a few additional options. Improvise with protectors to serve almost any purpose you have in mind.

Basket	Protector Combinations	Basket	Protector Combinations
Berry, Small	1 Tea	Market, Small (cont.)	8 Chives™
Berry, Medium	2 Small Key		2 Tea with 4 Chives™
	1 Tea		2 Recipe™ with 1 Medium Key
	4 Chives™		3 Recipe™
Bread or Bakery™	2 Medium Berry with 1 Bread WoodCrafts Divider	Market, Medium	2 Spring
			3 Medium Key
	1 Medium Berry with Small Covered Dish, Small 6" Mixing Bowl or Stackable Bowl		3 Tall Key
		Market, Large	3 Tall Key
	1 Spring with 1 Tea		2 Small Gathering (Stacked)
	3 Tea with 2 Bread WoodCrafts Dividers	Pantry™	*See* Gathering, Small
	6 Chives™ with 2 Bread WoodCrafts Dividers	Picnic, Small (with Wood Riser)	1 Cracker with 1 Medium Berry and 1 Tea
			3 Cracker
Cake (or Small Picnic without Wood Riser)	4 Small Key	Picnic, Large	2 Bread
	2 Cracker		2 Magazine
	4 Small Spoon		1 Magazine with 2 Large Spoon
Chore	4 Tea		4 Medium Spoon
Gathering, Small (or Pantry™)	4 Tea		3 Tall Key
	1 Large Berry	Pie	1 Cracker with 1 Medium Berry and 1 Medium Key
	2 Cracker		
Gathering, Medium	5 Medium Key		2 or 3 Cracker
	2 Large Berry		4 Small Key
	2 Spring (consider using 1 divided)	Serving Tray	2 Medium Berry with 2 Tea
	1 Cake Divider with 1 Spring Protector		4 Medium Berry with 3 Tea
Gathering, Large	2 Spring with 2 Medium Spoon		6 Small Berry
	8 Small Spoon		2 Bread with 2 Tea
Key, Medium	2 Chives™ 1 Cracker with Divider		1 Bread (divides basket down the middle)
Magazine	1 Medium Spoon		5 Cracker
	1 or 2 Large Spoon	Spring	2 Small Spoon
Market, Small	1 Large Berry with 2 Tea		2 Medium Key
	2 Large Berry		4 Chives™
	2 Medium Key with 2 Tea	Vegetable, Medium	1 Small Spoon with 1 Medium Spoon
	3 Tall Key		

Glossary of Cooking Techniques

Bake . . . . To cook by dry heat in an oven, or under hot coals.

Baste . . . . To moisten, especially meats, with melted butter, pan drippings, sauce, etc., during cooking time.

Beat . . . . To mix ingredients by vigorous stirring or with electric mixer.

Blanch . . . . . . To immerse, usually vegetables or fruit, briefly into boiling water to inactivate enzymes, loosen skin, or soak away excess salt.

Blend . . . . To combine 2 or more ingredients, at least 1 of which is liquid or soft, to quickly produce a mixture that has a smooth uniform consistency.

Boil . . . . To heat liquid until bubbly; the boiling point for water is about 212 degrees, depending on the altitude and the atmospheric pressure.

Braise . . . . . . To cook, especially meats, covered, in a small amount of liquid.

Broil . . . . To cook by direct exposure to intense heat such as a flame or an electric heating unit.

Caramelize . . To melt sugar in a heavy pan over low heat until golden brown, stirring constantly.

Chill . . . . To cool in the refrigerator or in cracked ice.

Cream . . . . . . To blend shortening, butter, or margarine, which usually has been softened, or sometimes oil, with a granulated or crushed ingredient until the mixture is soft and creamy. Usually described in method as light and fluffy.

Cut in . . . . . . To disperse solid shortening into dry ingredients with a knife or pastry blender. Texture of the mixture should resemble coarse cracker meal. Described in method as crumbly.

Deep-fry . . . . To cook in a deep pan or skillet containing hot cooking oil. Deep-fried foods are generally completely immersed in the hot oil.

Deglaze . . . . . To heat stock, wine, or other liquid in the pan in which meat has been cooked, mixing with pan juices and sediment to form a gravy or sauce base.

Degrease . . . . To remove accumulated fat from surface of hot liquids.

Dice . . . . To cut into small cubes about $1/4$ inch in size.

Dissolve . . . . To create a solution by thoroughly mixing a solid or granular substance with a liquid until no sediment remains.

Dredge . . . . . To coat completely with flour, bread crumbs, etc.

Fillet . . . . To remove bones from meat or fish. (Pieces of meat, fish, or poultry from which bones have been removed are called fillets.)

Fold in . . . . . . To blend a delicate frothy mixture into a heavier one so that none of the lightness or volume is lost. Using a rubber spatula, turn under and bring up and over, rotating bowl $1/4$ turn after each folding motion.

Fry . . . . To cook in a pan or skillet containing hot cooking oil. The oil should not totally cover the food.

Garnish . . . . . To decorate food before serving.

Glaze . . . . To cover or coat with sauce, syrup, egg white, or a jellied substance. After applying, it becomes firm, adding color and flavor.

Grate . . . . To rub food against a rough, perforated utensil to produce slivers, chunks, curls, etc.

Grill . . . . To broil, usually over hot coals or charcoal.

Grind . . . . To cut, crush, or force through a chopper to produce small bits.

Julienne . . . . To cut vegetables, fruit, etc., into long thin strips.

Knead . . . . . . To press, fold, and stretch dough until smooth and elastic.

Leaven . . . . . . To cause batters and doughs to rise, usually by means of a chemical leavening agent. This process may occur before or during baking.

Marinate . . . . To soak, usually in a highly seasoned oil-acid solution, to flavor and/or tenderize food.

Melt . . . . To liquefy solid foods by the action of heat.

Mince . . . . . . To cut or chop into very small pieces.

Mix . . . . To combine ingredients to distribute uniformly.

Mold . . . . To shape into a particular form.

Panbroil . . . . To cook in a skillet or pan using a very small amount of fat to prevent sticking.

Panfry . . . . . . To cook in a skillet or pan containing only a small amount of fat.

Parboil . . . . . To partially cook in boiling water. Most parboiled foods require additional cooking with or without other ingredients.

Pit . . . . To remove the hard inedible seed from peaches, plums, etc.

Plump . . . . . . To soak fruits, usually dried, in liquid until puffy and softened.

Preserve . . . . To prevent food spoilage by pickling, salting, dehydrating, smoking, boiling in syrup, etc. Preserved foods have excellent keeping qualities when properly prepared and stored.

Purée . . . . To reduce the pulp of cooked fruit and vegetables to a smooth and thick liquid by straining or blending.

Reduce . . . . . To boil stock, gravy, or other liquid until volume is reduced, liquid is thickened, and flavor is intensified.

Roast . . . . (1) To cook by dry heat either in an oven or over hot coals. (2) To dry or parch by intense heat.

Sauté . . . . To cook quickly in a skillet containing a small amount of hot cooking oil. Sautéed foods should never be immersed in the cooking oil and should be stirred frequently.

Scald . . . . (1) To heat a liquid almost to the boiling point. (2) To soak, usually vegetables or fruit, in boiling water until the skins are loosened; *see* Blanch.

Scallop . . . . . To bake with a sauce in a casserole. The food may either be mixed or layered with the sauce.

Score . . . . To make shallow cuts diagonally in parallel lines, especially in meat.

Scramble . . . To cook and stir simultaneously, especially eggs.

Shred . . . . To cut or shave food into slivers.

Shuck . . . . To remove the husk from corn or the shell from oysters, clams, etc.

Sieve . . . . To press a mixture through a closely meshed metal utensil to make it homogeneous.

Sift . . . . To pass, usually dry ingredients, through a fine wire mesh in order to produce a uniform consistency.

Simmer . . . . . To cook in or with a liquid at just below the boiling point.

Skewer . . . . . . (1) To thread, usually meat and vegetables, onto a sharpened rod (as in shish kabob). (2) To fasten the opening of stuffed fowl closed with small pins.

Skim . . . . To ladle or spoon off excess fat or scum from the surface of a liquid.

Steam . . . . . . To cook with water vapor in a closed container, usually in a steamer, on a rack, or in a double boiler.

Sterilize . . . . . To cleanse and purify through exposure to intense heat.

Stir-fry . . . . . To cook small pieces of vegetables and/or meat in a small amount of oil in a wok or skillet over high heat until tender-crisp, stirring constantly.

Strain . . . . To pass through a strainer, sieve, or cheesecloth to break down or remove solids or impurities.

Stuff . . . . To fill or pack cavities, especially those of meats, vegetables, and poultry.

Toast . . . . To brown and crisp, usually by means of direct heat, or to bake until brown.

Toss . . . . To mix lightly with lifting motion using 2 forks or spoons.

Truss . . . . To bind poultry legs and wings close to the body before cooking.

Whip . . . . To beat a mixture until air has been thoroughly incorporated and the mixture is light and fluffy, the volume is increased, and the mixture holds its shape.

Wilt . . . . To apply heat to cause dehydration, color change, and a droopy appearance.

Equivalents

	When the recipe calls for	Use
Baking	½ cup (1 stick) butter	4 ounces
	2 cups (4 sticks) butter	1 pound
	4 cups all-purpose flour	1 pound
	4½ cups sifted cake flour	1 pound
	1 square chocolate	1 ounce
	1 cup semisweet chocolate chips	6 ounces
	4 cups marshmallows	1 pound
	2¼ cups packed brown sugar	1 pound
	4 cups confectioners' sugar	1 pound
	2 cups sugar	1 pound
Cereal/Bread	1 cup fine dry bread crumbs	4 to 5 slices
	1 cup soft bread crumbs	2 slices
	1 cup small bread crumbs	2 slices
	1 cup fine saltine crumbs	28 saltines
	1 cup fine graham cracker crumbs	15 graham crackers
	1 cup vanilla wafer crumbs	22 wafers
	1 cup crushed cornflakes	3 cups uncrushed
	4 cups cooked macaroni	8 ounces uncooked
	3½ cups cooked rice	1 cup uncooked rice

	When the recipe calls for	Use
Dairy	1 cup shredded cheese	4 ounces
	1 cup cottage cheese	8 ounces
	1 cup sour cream	8 ounces
	1 cup whipped cream	½ cup heavy cream
	⅔ cup evaporated milk	1 (5⅓-ounce) can
	1⅔ cups evaporated milk	1 (13-ounce) can
Fruit	4 cups sliced or chopped apples	4 medium
	1 cup mashed bananas	3 medium
	2 cups pitted cherries	4 cups unpitted
	2½ cups shredded coconut	8 ounces
	4 cups cranberries	1 pound
	1 cup pitted dates	1 (8-ounce) package
	1 cup candied fruit	1 (8-ounce) package
	3 to 4 tablespoons lemon juice plus 1 tablespoon grated lemon zest	1 lemon
	⅓ cup orange juice plus 2 teaspoons grated orange zest	1 orange
	4 cups sliced peaches	8 medium
	2 cups pitted prunes	1 (12-ounce) package
	3 cups raisins	1 (15-ounce) package

Measurement Equivalents

1 tablespoon = 3 teaspoons	8 tablespoons = ½ cup	2 cups = 1 pint
2 tablespoons = 1 ounce	12 tablespoons = ¾ cup	4 cups = 1 quart
4 tablespoons = ¼ cup	16 tablespoons = 1 cup	4 quarts = 1 gallon
5 tablespoons + 1 teaspoon = ⅓ cup	1 cup = 8 ounces	

INDEX